Please, Somebody Love Me!

Jillian . . . thank you for sharing your powerful story with so much simplicity, sincerity, and love. Truly, you are allowing God to work in your life in a positive and dynamic way. What a splendid inspiration you are to all of us!

> Dr. Robert Harold Schuller
> Founder and Chairman of the Board
> The Crystal Cathedral, Garden Grove, California

When I first met Jillian . . . I had no idea of the pain her beauty hid . . . . She had worked to disguise her childhood insecurities and fears. As I read about God's healing power in her life, I feel honored to have been a part of that process. I know that the lives of many women will be touched through Jillian's transparency.

> Florence Littauer

. . . From an abandoned, heartbroken little girl, God orchestrated a loving adoption. From a frightened teen trapped in a world of insecurity, God graced a princess, full of beauty, poise, and charm. It is with this newfound strength, that Jillian now shares her story of a God who dreams big dreams for his children.

> Susie Shellenberger
> Editor, *Brio* magazine
> Focus on the Family

It's hard to believe that Jillian's story is everyone's story. She is so beautiful and talented and gifted that you catch your breath when you hear her say, "Will somebody please love me?" It is the world's autobiography, not just for the downtrodden, but also for the rich and famous and the high achievers. Read it!

> Dr. Bruce Larson
> Co-Pastor
> The Crystal Cathedral, Garden Grove, California

On the subject that is often given a clinical rather than a personal treatment, Jillian and co-writer, Joseph Ryan, have woven her experiences as an abused and unwanted child into a book that provides understanding and advice, as well as evidence of God's redeeming love.

> David Meece

Please, Somebody Love Me!

*Surviving Abuse
and Becoming Whole*

Jillian
and
Joseph A. Ryan

© 1991 by Jillian and Joseph A. Ryan

Published by Fleming H. Revell
a division of Baker Book House Company
P.O. Box 6287, Grand Rapids, MI 49516-6287

Spire edition published 1996

Printed in the United States of America

ISBN 0-8007-8640-8

Unless otherwise indicated, Scripture quotations are from the King James Version.

Scripture quotations identified RSV are from the Revised Standard Version of the Bible, copyright 1946, 1952, 1971, and 1973 by the Division of Christian Education of the National Council of the Churches of Christ in the United States of America.

To Joe and Velma Ryan,
my loving father and mother—my
greatest earthly treasure

Jillian, about two and one-half years old.

A Note from JILLIAN

Tomorrow I sign the final contract for *Please, Somebody Love Me!* I find myself on my knees searching for answers from my Father in heaven. "Why should I release my story? What are my reasons . . . my motives? Could it possibly help or encourage others?"

Then I remember the many faces of people who talk to me after my concerts, sharing their own pain and sorrow. So many are hurting, so are lonely, so many are on a never-ending search for love or forgiveness or approval. It's then I dare to believe that by publishing my own story I can somehow multiply my witness to God's mighty grace and power.

When I was in high school, I not only dreamed of being a singer; I wanted to write my story, too. Perhaps I did—in secret. I started writing poetic lines at age sixteen . . . remembering childhood events, the nightmares that repeated their same endless patterns, and longing so deeply to find some way I could express myself.

Years later, when I really did begin to write, when I wanted to let the world know what happened to me and what continues to happen to countless children all over the world, I couldn't imagine where I'd find the facts to bolster my memories, but in addition to the adoption agency's report, sources appeared which I knew nothing about.

Somehow a twenty-year-old tape I had made as a little girl surfaced and confirmed some memories of early years.

And I learned that Dad and Mother, each without knowing what the other was doing, had been storing away facts about me. Mother made notes on incidents over the years and put those bits and pieces in a shoebox. Dad kept a personal journal, and I appeared on many of those pages. Could it have been God's plan all along for this book to appear?

Though I have been quite frank in my writing, I have used restraint in giving details where others are directly involved. Names or locations have been changed in some instances to avoid hurting or embarrassing anyone.

I know that foster homes, child-care facilities, adoption agencies, and social workers, are a necessary part of society today. It is not my desire to discredit them. People who offer these services work hard for low pay, and many care deeply about their young charges. Nevertheless, my unhappy experiences were real—too real—and too painful.

My earnest desire is that this book will cause discussion in homes and churches about some often-ignored, but crucial, family and social issues. I want it to bring hope and healing to those who suffer as I did.

Most of all, I hope it will cause people to long for God's love in their lives and to see him as their only hope. He offers hope to a hurting world. How great God is!

Contents

Photo section follows page 64

Acknowledgments

How can I thank so many who have had such a special part in my life? Let me mention just a few:

My church family at First Church of the Nazarene in Nashville, whose support and love give me spiritual strength to keep going.

My pastor, John Denny, for holding me accountable and showing such confidence in me and in what I'm doing.

Mel McCullough, Rick Eastman, and the people at Bethany First Church in Oklahoma—I saw Jesus in you. Thank you for showing the unconditional love for one another that truly comes through a relationship with Christ.

So many pastors and wives around the country who support this ministry through prayer.

Pastor Marion McKellops in Phoenix—your humor and spiritual investment in my life continues to mean so much.

My recording company, for believing in my ministry.

Bill Meagher, a daily source of wisdom and direction in my life. Thank You!

Chuck Swindoll, who continues to be a spiritual teacher in my life through his tremendous books.

My friends, Florence and Marita Littauer, for reintroducing me to a God of healing power—a God of restoration.

Baker Book House, who believed my story could give others a source of hope.

Larry Bastain—one of the greatest songwriters I've ever known. Thank you for believing in me and showing how to put my "Best" into words.

Wes Yoder and the people at the Ambassador Agency.

Linda Mensch—for your guidance and support.

Jim Pederic—thank you for "My Gift."

Angela Bowers—you are always there for me. I love you so much—can't wait to be in heaven with you.

Shirley Dougan, another special person and prayer warrior in my life.

Bob and Emily Barnes, for encouraging me to write this book. You knew it was a story that needed to be told.

Susie Shellenberger—I love you and will meet you at six o'clock for pizza!

Kent and Barbara Bull, my dear friends in Phoenix.

Anita Bryant and Charlie—Anita, you have become my friend, and our hearts have been melted together through similar experiences.

David Meece—you were my favorite Christian artist as I grew up. I admire you. We need more artists with your transparency. Thank you for your voice to the world.

Marion Schlesinger, who helped build a foundation for love where there was none in my confused childhood world.

My grandparents, for waiting twenty-four years and never giving up hope that someday I would find them.

My friends at Temple Baptist Church in Portland, Oregon— though I didn't realize it growing up, you did see me through. Special thanks to Fran Maynard who gave me the courage to sing.

Robert Schuller and Bruce Larson for their inspiration and gentle loving spirit.

Pat Robertson and the 700 Club for their work in ministering to the hurting lives around the world. Thank you for telling my story.

Ed and Rebecca Erwin—we love you.

Pastor Howard Boyd and Cathy, for your love and friendship.

Rob, for your never ending encouragement, and your dreams that continually push me on. I love you.

Jerry Rose—to you and your family at Channel 38, thanks for your love and friendship.

Uncle Noel—for keeping the wheels turning.

To so many friends who remain unnamed. You have touched my life, and I hold a place for you in my heart.

Foreword

I met Jillian in Chicago at a telethon for Channel 38. It was an instantaneous kinship of spirits and I loved her. It was as if we had known each other for many years.

Later when Jillian asked me to write a foreword to her life story, I happily accepted and eagerly awaited the manuscript. As I read of her roots I was reading my own story. We both came to Christ at eight years of age. Jillian's relentless, uninhibited "performances" for friends, family, or anyone who would listen, as part of her struggle to be accepted and loved, sounded just like me. I, too, experienced childhood molestation, a fact I have never publicly acknowledged. Later, as an adult I suffered continual verbal abuse. Abuse is devastating and causes deep wounds, some visible, some invisible.

Most of us have not experienced the total devastation and dark depths of Jillian's pain, rejection, and anger. If we're really honest, however, there is a little frightened Jill in each of us at some level. We seek and hope, "Please, somebody love me."

God's grace and loving mercy can uncover, comfort, and heal the hidden bruises that scar our lives. Thank God for those true Christian friends and counselors who can love unconditionally and help us pray for inner healing by forgiving those who hurt us. As Jillian says, "Abused people need to know that healing after damage does not come with a snap of the fingers. Forgiving takes time. Working through memories takes time. There is a recovery period and that's acceptable."

Anita Bryant

Preface

He was a six-year-old boy—just another child in a foster home. This family was selected with the boy's good in mind by his widowed father, who was leaving for a distant job. But the best intentions don't always guarantee the best results.

The bare, isolated attic assigned as the boy's sleeping space confirmed his feeling that the family thought of him as an outsider.

Bladder pressure awakened him one night, commanding, "Get up!" Because there were no attic lights or handrail by the narrow, steep stairs, he slowly and carefully slid his body down the dark steps. But before he could find his way across open space to the bathroom, his bladder emptied.

The next morning—Judgment Day! The woman condemned him as naughty and wicked, then rubbed his nose and face in the pool of urine. To be sure his crime would not be repeated, she sent the boy back to his attic space to await further punishment.

The man thundered up the steps with rope in hand. He bound the boy's feet together with one end. A quick wrist-flip by the man sent the other end of the rope over a rafter, and he grabbed it when it fell. By pulling on the rope, he slowly lifted the boy's feet higher and higher into the air until his head cleared the floor. He anchored the rope's free end. The boy dangled like a side of beef swaying in a butcher shop.

The blood rushed to his head. Frantically, he watched the face of his tormentor slowly disappear down the stairs. He was alone. Unconsciousness soon swallowed his fear. Whether seconds or minutes went by, he never knew. Eventually someone came to take him down. Like millions of other abused children, he survived. In his case, there are no scars the eye can see.

She was a seven-year-old girl who endured not just one but many such homes and experiences—some of them much worse. The boy was now a forty-seven-year-old man. He sat in a small room with his wife and son, looking through a huge two-way mirror in a Los Angeles adoption agency. He watched intently as that little girl talked and played.

She was lithe and graceful. Her olive skin, chestnut hair, and an expressive Middle Eastern face set with large choco-late eyes combined to make her unusually attractive. Later it became evident that her outward beauty thinly veiled a tur-bulent inner life—seething with fiery anger, bubbling with laughter, or running deep with rivers of love, poetry, and song.

Forty years apart in age, Jillian, you and I were linked as dad and daughter by court decree. You didn't know it then, but some of that link was forged by the partial similarity of our childhoods. I understood you. For much of the fourteen years we lived together, I saw more of your hot anger than the laughter, love, and song. But early in that time you received my Savior, Jesus Christ. God loved you through those years, and we both survived.

How grateful I am now as I see your healing and growth in God's grace. Pride and joy mingle as I watch your min-istry of music and testimony across the country. The fiery crucible of your childhood and early adult years has formed the powerful bond of understanding between you and bat-tered women. And you understand the cries of the world's deprived children.

That you followed me in a ministry with World Vision can be ascribed only to the sovereign plan of God for this part of your life. Your success in personally getting thousands of sponsors for boys and girls the world over is a fulfillment of "In everything God works for good" (Rom. 8:28 RSV). The hurts in your life now bring praise and glory to God in others' lives and joy to your own.

May God's love so flood your life that your concert ministry will always come from the overflow of your heart. May *Please, Somebody Love Me* work together with your music albums to let many know you, though they've never met you. More than anything, may they come to know your Jesus, too.

I love you.
Dad

1

Love Betrayed

"Love must be sincere." Romans 12:9

The bright red Fierro's tires fight frantically to hold the curves of the rain-slick road. Yet I accelerate even more, anxious to put as much mileage as possible between David and me.

The pounding Oregon rain has almost erased the marker lines on the night road. They are practically invisible to me.

I envy those little lines; I want to be invisible, too. Nonexistent. If only I could disappear—get away from the haunting hurts and continuing pain we call living.

"Hell must be better than this," I scream into the night air. "Lord, how could you let this happen . . . again?"

The sobs erupt from so deep within me that my entire body shakes—as though someone were trying to wrench out a part of my stomach.

I drive automatically . . . ever faster . . . without thinking

. . . conscious thoughts totally on my pain . . . bleeding inside . . . wanting to disappear . . . or die.

I shout furiously at God, "Why did you allow me to get stuck in another tormenting relationship?"

At the same time, I am furious at myself, moaning, "I'd do almost anything for love, but how could I be so stupid? How could I let another man hurt me so much?" Tears run down my cheeks, etching random patterns in my makeup.

I pound the steering wheel with my shaking fist and repeat, "Hell's *got* to be better than this."

The next moment, my sports car hydroplanes and spins uncontrollably across the slippery bridge, finally crashing into the guard rail. It catches my car like a net and leaves me suspended, in shambles, one hundred feet above the swirling river.

The force of the accident leaves me helpless—in shock.

Unable to move.

Suspended in time.

Trapped.

"I can't believe I'm still alive," I whisper, knowing I am not strong enough to take my own life, but wishing I could have been "lucky enough" to have the accident do it for me.

Instead, I am momentarily held captive in a crushed steel cage at one o'clock in the morning, forced to think about many things, especially the haunting scene that was engraved on my mind only thirty minutes before. . . .

Earlier that evening, my life seemed to be going in a positive direction. After finding a new modeling job, I sped home and parked my car in the driveway. I was eager to unwind by spending some time with David.

David! Hope and expectancy lightened every step as I dashed up the few stairs leading to our first-floor condominium.

Oh, I admit that I hesitated to give up my modeling career in California, move back to Oregon, and start over again with new friends and business associates.

But David was so persistent. Finally, he convinced me that

20   *Please, Somebody Love Me!*

he desperately wanted me to be with him in Oregon. He made me believe that my moving to Oregon was the best way for us to get a fresh start . . . for our love to grow and be nurtured.

It was a personal sacrifice, a calculated risk, but I felt in my heart that David was worth it.

And with each step toward the condo, I believed David was right. All our difficulties were now a fading memory as I walked through that door, anxious to rebuild my life with David.

But when I walked into the living room, an explosion of rocketing emotions shattered my romantic dreams.

David was already there, sitting on the couch, with *him*—his former lover.

But it couldn't be!

David had promised me it was all over! He had said it would never happen again . . . that he loved me so much . . . that I made him forget his desire for men.

So what was *he* doing here now . . . invading my home? Hadn't David told me, "Jillian, I've found God's healing power and have experienced his forgiveness. That's now a part of my past"? Yet there the past was . . . sitting on the couch.

The emotions of that moment slashed my soul, and with it every part of my new life.

I was bleeding.

Abused.

Tricked.

Betrayed.

If the deep wounds of that moment had been slashes on my body instead of my heart, David would have been thrown into prison for the mutilation he inflicted. Instead, it was I who was tossed into a prison . . . of confused emotions.

I wanted to scream something at David, to say something that would give some sense to this senseless situation. But there were no words. All that came out of my mouth was, "How could you do this to me? How could you? How could you?"

I hated him.

And I hated Jillian.

Surely my figure must not be good enough. My face must not be pretty enough. My love for him must not be deep enough or strong enough. If I was really lovable, none of this would have happened!

Oh, how I wanted to hide. But where could I run to conceal my shame?

I ran out of the living room, down the stairs, out the front door, and into the pelting Oregon rain, which immediately soaked my hair and my dress.

But I didn't care.

The harsh rain only stung my skin.

David had stung my soul.

Somewhere in my foggy emotional trance I heard him screaming behind me . . . his words muffled by the chaos in my mind.

I glanced back at his face and saw tears streaming down. His mouth moved with words I could barely hear. But the tears were not enough, and the words were empty.

"Jillian, stop. Please, come back. I promise you—it's really over this time."

"Like you promised before?" I wondered.

"I love *you*," he shouted.

"But not enough to keep you away from *him*," I thought.

"I know I have a problem. But I'll get help. Please come back. . . ."

I had no feelings left, except for the desire to escape.

I'd heard David's worthless words before—again and again! And not only from him, but from others in my life who had said "I love you"—then stabbed my unprotected heart.

Fumbling and stumbling, I made it into my car, leaving David behind with his tears, his words, and his friend.

And then, as I drove away, old memories of a little girl began to surface and haunt me again. Memories of times so tormenting that I often tried to hide them . . . to stuff them away . . . to forget.

Please, Somebody Love Me!

But I couldn't hide them this time.

David had just broken open the safe storage places in my heart. Now the old memories of little Jill were oozing out in uncontrollable patterns of pain.

"Lord," I cried, "how did it get to be so bad? Where did I go so wrong? What did I do to deserve such treatment? Why am I not good enough for the men I love?"

While I was driving, I glanced at my reflection in the rearview mirror. The reality of my tear-stained face startled me. I looked horrible. Hours before, my makeup was perfectly in place. That is something I have learned to do well—to cover up. A cover girl—that's it. I had spent the last few years professionally covering up as a successful high-fashion model.

A perfect face, a designer dress, beautiful shoes, jewelry that hung like ornaments—this is what people see when I model.

But where is little Jill?

"Chin up! Now walk out and face your crowd."

But where is little Jill?

"Oh, you look so beautiful. Jillian, you are perfect, absolutely perfect."

If they only knew.

As I sit in my smashed Fierro, I can hear myself saying:

"Little Jill, stay away from me. You can't come out. There's no place for you in my life. I'm successful now. And up to a few minutes ago I thought I had everything I wanted. So just stay away. I don't want you. Your presence hurts too much. Don't come back—ever again."

Little Jill has too much emotional luggage to carry along in the journey of life. I'm "Jillian" now.

But though I've tried to lock Jill away in a distant corner of my shattered heart, that insecure, battered little girl has escaped again. And it's going to be easier to release myself from this wrecked car than to release little Jill from my buried memories.

Little Jill's insistent cry, a cry impossible for me to ignore, begins to plead her case for love and approval once again . . .

> Please, somebody love me;
> Try, if you can.
> Look into my eyes,
> See if you understand.
>
> I'm not a bad person;
> I just don't like being me.
> If we could trade, you know I would,
> But you wouldn't like being me.

2

"Jill, Go Get Your Suitcase"

*"Though my father and mother forsake me,
the Lord will receive me." Psalm 27:10*

Mama, can you hear me?
I'm your daughter from a long time ago.
Well, if you don't remember, I'm not surprised;
You gave me away when I was a couple of years old.

Mama, I wish you could see me.
I think you'd be proud of the person they call *me*.
I'm young, pretty, talented, I'm told.
But most of all, Mama, inside of me
There's a part of you that neglected to leave.

Mama, I wish you could touch me,
Take me in your arms and hold me secure.
You see, when you left, that's
Something you took along with you,
So now when I'm loved, I'm not so sure.

Mama, some day I'll find you, and
You can see for yourself what your
Little girl has grown up to be.
But in the meantime, when I
Dream or think or wish,
I'll just think of you as someone
Who's part of me.

(Written at age sixteen)

It wasn't until I reached the age of four that I realized I was different from other children. I had a tattered little cardboard suitcase that I carried from home to home. Sometimes it took only a knock on the door. Other times the phone would ring. Then someone would come in and tell me to pack my suitcase. It was time to leave and move on.

So many strangers . . . so many faces . . . I never knew who my next mommy or daddy would be. You see, they called me a "foster child." Little did I realize when I first got my little suitcase, that before I reached the age of eight I would journey in and out of twelve different foster homes—homes sometimes filled with terror for a little child and often with abuse that would affect my life forever.

I don't think I was different when I was born. In fact, what little I have learned of my first year sounds normal. The birth certificate says my lungs drew their first breath in the hospital of a coastal community next to Los Angeles. I was a pre-Christmas baby, born 22 December, the second child of young, immature-though-married parents.

The pregnancy was uneventful. When they put me on the scales at birth, I weighed seven pounds. I fed at my mama's breast for two months before she started me on solids. By the seventh month, I was crawling and cutting teeth; at eight months, I took my first steps. At the end of my first year of life, understandable words were beginning to tumble out of my mouth.

What was going on in my mother's and father's lives during that time? Did they love me? Were there quarrels? Did their yelling frighten me into my own infant screams? Was my daily care too much for them? Did they resent my arrival? Was I unplanned?

Even today, I don't know the answers to all those questions. But I do know that at the end of that first year of life my parents separated, abandoning me and my two-year-old brother, Jon, to a seventy-year-old widow in downtown Los Angeles. The woman gave me little care with no affection, leaving me in my crib all day.

It was from this home that Jon and I came under the care of a private adoption agency in Los Angeles when I was two years and three months old. When I was received by the agency the social worker described me as "emotionally starved." To a child, that meant feeling inside like famine victims look on the outside. But if you had been there you'd also have seen my matted, dirty hair and the ugly impetigo sores covering my body. Soon I began having seizures—diagnosed much later as being caused by "emotional deprivation."

So it was that when I was two years old, my suitcase and I began our journey.

In the blur of those many foster homes, I remember mainly the periodic episodes of pain. Those episodes left not only physical scars, but deep emotional ones the eyes cannot see.

One foster home belonged to a policeman and his family who had a playhouse in the backyard. That playhouse was so big and painted so pretty that to me it looked like a beautiful castle I'd seen in a fairy-tale book. When I first arrived at the policeman's home, he took me out to the playhouse, pointed to it, and said, "Now Jill, you can play anywhere else in the yard you want, but you are forbidden to play here. Monsters live in there, and if you go in, they'll kill you! So you must stay away."

He sounded so concerned for me. "Jill, watch out for the monsters!"

But even as a little girl, I felt that all the policeman really cared about was that I might mess up that playhouse, which he had built for his real daughter. Watching her was my only privilege while she laughed and played in the little house with all the neighbor children. I could never understand why I wasn't invited.

One day, when no one seemed to be around, I couldn't resist going inside the playhouse. But almost immediately the policeman appeared. I had reason to feel uneasy. From the moment I met him, I had sensed he was a mean man. He couldn't just talk; he yelled at everyone. Now his stern and angry face frightened me. And soon I learned how cruel he could be to a child.

"Jill, I told you *never* to come in here! Don't ever disobey my orders. You will stay outside tonight . . . in the backyard. I'm going to lock you out of the house and see how you like staying in the dark with the monsters."

He kept his word. That night, I sat shaking on the lawn of their dark backyard. I remember knocking on the back door a few times, but no one ever answered. I didn't sleep at all. And I never went into that playhouse again.

During that time, even in my child-mind, rules for living as a foster child began to take shape:

> RULE ONE: NO MATTER WHAT YOU ARE TOLD, YOU ARE NEVER EQUAL TO THE OTHER CHILDREN IN THE FAMILY. THEY WILL ALWAYS BE ALLOWED TO DO THINGS YOU CANNOT DO.

At first, my brother Jon and I were kept together. He was my only real family, my only security. I clung to him desperately. We used to talk together and hold each other for comfort. But that didn't last long.

One day I came home from an errand with my foster mother, the policeman's wife, and sat down on the floor in the living room to watch TV with Jon. The program had just begun when "mother" said, "Jill, you need to go upstairs and pack your suitcase. You're going away for the weekend to stay with your grandparents" (my foster mother's parents).

I went upstairs, put some things in my suitcase, and then gave Jon a big good-bye hug. After I was driven to the other house, I unpacked what I brought and waited for the weekend to be over. When the time came, I asked when I was going home. They simply replied, "Didn't anyone tell you? You're staying here." And so I was separated from my brother.

The adoption agency's records reported that experience this way:

> In the ensuing months which involved casework with the children, the decision was made that in permanent planning, the children should be separated because of the interplay of their personalities and the dynamics of their interpersonal and parental roles.

Even as an adult, I don't know what that means. What I experienced at the young age of four was being taken away from Jon without warning and tossed to a new family. I felt betrayed.

My new home "mommy and daddy" were the parents of the "mother" in the previous home. Often, the families would visit together. But on each visit, they would make me stay in the car with the windows rolled up.

"Jill, we want you to stay in the car," they would say, without any explanation. "Be a good girl. You will be very naughty if you try to talk to Jon."

But that did not stop me from "seeing" my brother. He would sneak out the back door of the house, come to the car, stretch up his arm, and put his hand on the window. I'd try to touch his hand by matching it thumb to thumb, fingers to fingers, on my side of the glass, as the tears ran down my cheeks.

Over the next few weeks, this scene was repeated several times. The glass always reminded us that we were forever separate.

To this day, I cannot explain why they did not want Jon and me together, even for visits.

Finally, after four or five times, I didn't see Jon again.

RULE TWO: YOUR FAMILY IS NOT AS IMPORTANT AS A REAL FAMILY. REAL FAMILIES DO NOT SPLIT UP BROTHERS AND

SISTERS. BUT IN YOUR WORLD, IT'S OKAY TO SPLIT THEM UP
AND EVEN TEASE THEM BY NOT LETTING THEM EVEN TALK
OR TOUCH. PEOPLE CAN BE VERY CRUEL AND ARE NOT TO
BE TRUSTED.

I tried to cope with the embarrassment of wetting the bed
when I was young. Most of my foster parents seemed to
think I did it out of laziness. And several of my "mothers"
felt that they knew the cure for my "problem."

On my sixth birthday, I had wet my pants the night before.

"Just for that, young lady, you'll wear a diaper at your
birthday party," said my foster mother.

How can I forget my humiliation?

At the party, I received a pink stuffed pig that I named
Piggy. I poured out my hurts and tears to Piggy on that day
and held him privately in my room, crying into his soft fur.
Piggy took Jon's place as someone to talk to and to hold
when I felt bad.

Another mother came up with a different solution for my
bedwetting.

"Jill, I've had it with your wetting the bed," she told me,
"and I'm gonna make you stop once and for all." Her eyes
glared with hatred.

I stood speechless, waiting to be hit. What followed made
me wish I had been hit instead.

"Now take those pants off this minute," she snapped.

"Yes, ma'am," I replied in my scared little voice.

"Now, you lazy little thing, I'll teach you to wet the bed!
Take those pants and pull them down over your head. And
do it now!"

Locked in temporary shock by her command, I couldn't
move.

"You heard me. Put those panties over your head this
minute."

"But . . . " It was no use trying to object.

She shouted once more, "Do it now!"

So I did.

She made me walk around the house all day with my

30   *Please, Somebody Love Me!*

smelly underwear over my head. Oh, how it reeked with the smell of ammonia.

To this day the smell of ammonia makes me sick.

Another "mommy" told me, "If you keep wetting your bed, I'm going to put snails in it." In Southern California, unless a lot of snail bait is used, yards have armies of snails—with and without shells.

That woman knew very well that there was nothing I was more afraid of than snails. I didn't like to play in the back-yard because of them.

One morning I awoke to that familiar smell of ammonia. Terror filled my heart as I lifted the sheets to find slimy snails crawling around me!

I screamed. No one came.

RULE THREE: IT'S OKAY FOR PEOPLE TO DO HORRIBLE THINGS TO YOU, BECAUSE YOU'RE DIFFERENT FROM OTHER PEOPLE.

Once, when I was living with another family, I was rid-ing in the back of a truck with the other children. The truck had no tailgate.

One of the children, perhaps out of jealousy, perhaps out of boredom, thought it would be funny to push me out the back of the truck while it was moving.

I fell out and cracked my head on the pavement. When the truck stopped, the driver rushed to my rescue and car-ried me to the cab where I rode to the house. Perhaps if I'd been taken to a hospital or a doctor's office I wouldn't have been left with this scar on my head.

The boy who intentionally pushed me out of the truck was never punished.

RULE FOUR: OTHER CHILDREN CAN DO THINGS TO YOU THAT YOU ARE NOT ALLOWED TO DO TO THEM OR TO THEIR REAL BROTHERS AND SISTERS. HURT YOU. PUSH YOU. BE UNFAIR TO YOU. NONE OF IT MATTERS. THEY WILL NEVER BE PUNISHED.

I remember the "mommy" with the thick glasses that grotesquely magnified her eyes into foreboding spots on her face.

She terrified me.

One day when I was sitting on the floor, putting a picture puzzle together, I could not figure out where a particular piece went.

Suddenly the woman with those magnified eyes grabbed me, angrily shook my body, then pulled me over to the edge of the room, where she violently slammed my face into the sharp corner of a wall.

A large split opened down my forehead and dribbled blood. Even today, when I don't have makeup on, you can easily see the scar.

While that woman was banging my head, she was screaming at me, "You stupid little girl. You hopeless girl. Can't you do anything right? How can you be so pathetic?"

Then she grabbed me again and dragged me into the bathroom, where she shoved my head under the shower. In my young mind, I was sure she was actually trying to drown me.

I was screaming . . . gagging . . . trying to breathe . . . couldn't get any air.

The next day, it was obvious from her behavior that "mommy" was afraid I'd tell my social worker how she had treated me. For the next week after her violent outbreak, to try to make up for her behavior, she let me have my bed in the living room where I could watch TV, and she fed me candy.

RULE FIVE: SOMETIMES ABUSE IS GOOD. LET THEM HIT AND HURT YOU. THEN THEY'LL FEEL SORRY FOR YOU AFTERWARD, AND YOU'LL GET SOME ATTENTION AND TREATS.

In one home, I had to fight to belong. They did everything for their natural daughter. I felt like an outcast.

The rules of the home were different for me than for their child.

For example, I was under strict orders to come home

from school within ten minutes after the final bell rang. I had to be at our front door then—or else!

On the Friday before Mother's Day I stayed late after school for about a half hour to finish my Mother's Day present. "Father" was so angry about my coming home late from school that he would not listen to any excuse.

That night he made me sleep in the doghouse.

RULE SIX: FOSTER CHILDREN ARE THE SAME AS ANIMALS.

Couldn't anyone love me? Why did all this happen to me? How could it get any worse?

It not only could; it did . . . soon . . . and through so much of my life.

> Jon, do you remember
> The days of our childhood play—
> Any of the laughter or any of the tears
> That might have come our way?
>
> Jon, do you remember
> What it was like moving around
> To all the homes with the different strangers?
> Did it ever tear you down?
>
> Jon, do you remember
> Perhaps a parent's face,
> Maybe my mother nursing me,
> Or did someone else take her place?
>
> Jon, do you remember
> The day they split us apart?
> Please tell me I'm not the only one
> Who remembers a broken heart.
>
> (Dedicated to my brother Jon
> —written at age nineteen)

3

Dreaming of My Forever Home

"Love never fails." 1 Corinthians 13:8

    I couldn't understand why I was set apart from other children—why I was never good enough to have my own mommy and daddy. I remember that in many of my foster homes I'd find a couch or chair where I could sit, waiting and watching the front door.

I would tell myself, "Now Jill, if you're a real good girl—if you do everything just right—I bet you'll see your mommy and daddy come right through that front door. They'll grab your hand and take you home to be with them."

I waited . . . but my mother and father never came. So I began to fantasize about a place I called my "forever home" . . . a home with my very own mother and father . . . with dolls and toys to play with . . . a place I'd never have to leave again.

When I was two years old, after my father and mother gave the adoption agency custody, the agency had assigned a social worker to be responsible for me. I don't know how many social workers there were during the next six years. Perhaps it was Mrs. Schlesinger's warm smile and gentle affection that made her the only one I remember.

Agency rules required that I see her regularly. If my Wednesday afternoon visits had been a TV film scene, we'd have had the world's record for the number of retakes. I'd race down the hallway to her door. She would answer my knock, wrap me up in her arms, and give me a big kiss on my cheek. Then she'd place me in her chair.

I'd look up at her, ready to ask my eternal question: "Mrs. Schlesinger, have you found my forever home?"

Each time the answer was the same, "No, Jill, not yet, but I'm sure I will very soon."

The following visit, we would replay our parts. It was a long time before we made the final retake of that scene.

Near the end of my kindergarten year my dream of a forever home appeared to be turning into reality.

Mrs. Schlesinger told me about a family that wanted me. She must have said many other things about them, but all I cared at the moment was that someone *wanted* me.

So she and I and my foster family made plans for the move. Even though there had been some rough times with this last foster family, the Martins, it wasn't easy to leave them. I had been there longer than any other place—perhaps a year or so. At least, I knew what I had. But this new home was an unknown. Would it be like all the others?

The adoption agency record says the day was 25 May, but all I knew was that I was going to my forever home. When it came time to say goodbye to "Mama" Martin, "Daddy," and "Grandmother," who lived next door, my tears were real. I knew I would miss them. And I was scared of what was ahead.

Mrs. Schlesinger drove me in her car as she had so often done in the past, my suitcase again on the back seat. For once I didn't feel like talking, and she seemed to understand.

In my own mind I kept trying to say my new family's name right—Romero.

When we arrived at my new address, Mrs. Schlesinger took my hand and walked me to the door. "Mama" Martin had helped me pick a bouquet of flowers before we left. So when the Romeros opened the door, I smiled and handed the flowers to my new mother.

Things were different in this home. They really did want me. They even gave me my own bedroom, with my own dolls and toys. On Saturdays when I woke up, I'd run in and sit on my new daddy's lap. That was the day he'd give me my twenty-five cents allowance. Then, after breakfast, my new brother Bobby would let me ride on the back of his bike, and together we would hit the dime store for some candy.

This family did lots of interesting things. I learned to swim at the YWCA; during that hot Southern California summer we swam almost every day. We took wonderful drives to the beach and to the mountains and had family picnics in the park. I made friends easily in the neighborhood. I loved being part of a family and felt like I belonged. Yes, finally, my forever home.

Their plan was to adopt me.

Unfortunately, I soon learned about another part of life. My new brother, Bobby, seemed awfully big to me; they said he was twelve. From the beginning, I didn't feel completely at ease with him.

One day, when I was alone in my room, Bobby came in to play with me. At first, his play was innocent and fun. Then he started to feel my body in places I knew it was wrong to do. I felt very uncomfortable.

"Jill, take off your clothes so we can play doctor," he told me.

"Do I have to?" I asked, not wanting to argue with my new brother, yet not feeling right about his demand.

"Of course you do, silly. That's the way you play doctor," he said with authority.

He obviously knew how to play doctor, and I didn't. I finally agreed and took off my clothes.

When Bobby was done with his "doctor's examination," I felt humiliated and ashamed. Without saying anything, he left me alone on the bed and walked out of the room, leaving me to grab a sheet to cover my trembling body.

Even with Piggy there to talk to, I felt so alone. I don't know where "Mama" was then or during the other times it happened afterward.

Later, after I had dressed and washed my face, I remember thinking, "I wish I could run and hide. This isn't right. Doesn't he love me like my new mommy and daddy do? Why do I feel so upset?"

My new mother had told me when I first arrived, "Jill, if you ever need anything, you can always come to me. I'll be here for you." I believed her. And though I felt terribly ashamed inside, I knew I needed her help. So one evening when she was alone, I went in and sat next to her.

"Mama," I said, "I need to talk to you," and I began to tell her what Bobby had been doing. Through her tears, she said, "Jill, I'm so sorry. I promise you this will never happen again." She kept her word. It didn't happen again.

About a week later, Mama came to me with these words: "Jill, I'm very sorry, but we are not going to be able to keep you. Things are just not working out. Let's go to your room and pack your things. Mrs. Schlesinger will be here soon."

My "yes, ma'am," came out automatically. By now I was too well programmed to argue with "big people."

With each step toward my room, more rules for living— this time as an adopted child—began to form in my mind.

RULE ONE: YOU ARE NEVER AS IMPORTANT AS THE *REAL* FAMILY MEMBERS, EVEN IF SOMEONE WANTS TO ADOPT YOU.

RULE TWO: IF THERE'S EVER A PROBLEM, YOU'D BETTER KEEP QUIET ABOUT IT. IF YOU TELL, YOU'LL HAVE TO LEAVE THAT HOME, TOO.

RULE THREE: NEVER TRUST ANOTHER "MOMMY" OR "DADDY" WITH YOUR REAL FEELINGS.

Please, Somebody Love Me!

RULE FOUR: BECAUSE YOU ARE NOT THEIR OWN CHILD, YOU WILL NEVER BE A TRUE PART OF THEIR FAMILY, AND YOU WILL BE IMPOSSIBLE TO LOVE.

Today, when I read Mrs. Schlesinger's report on that sad experience, I realize she is writing it in professional jargon that takes out all the feelings and hurt. Here is how she entered it in the record I now have:

> Jill's adoptive placement broke down when their son, age twelve, became acutely disturbed and could not cope with the inclusion of a sibling. . . . The whole family functioning deteriorated. . . . She [Jill] says "Bobby was not able to be a brother."

It all ended just three months after I arrived at the Romeros. So it was back to the Martins for me—back to people I knew. They welcomed me with a party and were very kind. We never talked about what happened. I was just a foster child again.

Once more, speaking of the time after the Romeros, Mrs. Schlesinger wrote in her report: "Jill's social functioning and social progress during this period [back at the Martins] were clearly evidenced. The foster family speak of this . . . in spite of the sadness and disappointment involved."

It all sounds so clean, so clinical, so detached. Professional people's words couldn't measure or describe the depth of my feelings or what was really happening inside me. Probably they never knew all the evil that scarred me in some of the foster homes. Like most children anywhere in the world who are abused, I didn't tell.

After all . . . who believes a foster child?

If you'd been with us on the way back to the Martins, you'd have seen my underpants flapping like a flag from the car antenna. Before we got home, the pants were dry, and she stopped to let me put them back on.

She acted more like my mother than any of the women who called themselves "mommy" to me.

She was my only hope. And she wouldn't give up trying to find my forever home.

A year drifted by after the Romeros sent me back to be a foster child. Another scar of rejection was healing. I was now a second grader, not quite eight years old.

"Jill," Mrs. Schlesinger began after my welcome kiss on one of my regular visits, "Would you please go into the playroom and play something very quietly? I'll be there in just a bit."

But "quietly" wasn't in my play vocabulary. Down the hall and into the playroom I ran. There I darted for my favorite toy—a bright-red fire engine, big enough to ride. Once inside, I started pedaling out the door and back down the hall, squeezing the bulb of the airhorn to let everyone know I was there.

Mrs. Schlesinger quickly appeared, saying, "Oh, Jill, What am I going to do with you? How about a game of checkers?"

I didn't like playing checkers with Mrs. Schlesinger. She always won!

But I picked up the checker game and began to arrange it on the table. Just then the huge mirror on the wall caught my attention; I saw myself moving in it. For a quick minute I stood looking at my body from head to toe and turning my head from side to side. I picked up a piece of chalk and pretended I was putting makeup on my eyebrows and lips.

How could I possibly know that this was a two-way mirror with a hidden microphone on my side—and that on the other side a family was observing me?

When Mrs. Schlesinger came in we sat down to play. She was winning, as usual. Soon, she complained that there was a draft and went to close the door. While her back was

Please, Somebody Love Me!

turned, I slid one of my checkers clear across the board and yelled, "Crown me."

At that very moment, on the other side of the mirror, a Baptist minister named Joe Ryan smiled a big smile and whispered to his wife, Velma, "That's my girl!" He quickly decided that, though she had done some mischievous cheating, a girl who could think that fast and had that much spunk was a determined survivor.

On my next visit, when Mrs. Schlesinger answered my knock on her door, I knew something had happened. Before I could say anything she hugged me close; I could feel her tears as she kissed my cheek. Then she said the words I'd waited so many years to hear,

"Jill . . . my dear little Jill, I have the greatest news for you. I've found your 'forever home'!"

Somehow, I knew this time it was for real. I was going to have my own mommy and daddy. Someone really did want me.

Little did I realize this was the start of a beautiful plan—a plan only God could create for my future.

Once again I said good-bye to the Martins and to my neighborhood friends while Mrs. Schlesinger packed my things. (I was down to a cardboard box by this time.) Mrs. Schlesinger picked me up and we drove from Southern California's San Fernando Valley to La Habra, an hour away in Orange County.

The week before, I had had a hamburger with the Ryans at their home while their social worker and mine went to a restaurant. My parents tell me I was super careful with my napkin and tried so hard to do everything just right. This was the first home in my eight years of life that I remember being expected to use silverware. Others had always let me eat with my hands or use my fingers. As I think back now, it makes me angry that no one cared enough to teach me.

That first visit had been such a short one. But I guess we had all felt okay about it because now, on this sunny morning, I was on my way to my forever home.

We parked in front of the house. As I walked toward the door, my new dad opened it to take a picture of me. I dodged and bobbed, making a blurry picture . . . its blur perhaps a symbol of the day's memories.

There were quick hugs. Then I blurted out, "I saw a snake in the ivy by the curb!"

They mumbled something about "imagination."

In a sinking flash I thought, "Won't these people believe me either?" (The next day Mom flooded the ivy with water, and out came the snake!)

It was one of the happiest days of my life, but also one of the saddest. When Mrs. Schlesinger's familiar form moved down the walk to her car, she turned and waved to me. The pain in my heart was real; here was the one person I could always count on, leaving me. In my young mind I knew I would never forget her. She would always remain in my heart.

From the front door I looked straight across the white-carpeted living room to sliding glass doors that opened to a covered patio. I ran to survey the landscaped backyard. It was covered with green, cloverlike dichondra and surrounded by the usual Southern California brick wall.

"Is this where I'll play?" I asked.

"Yes, this is your yard, where you can have your friends over to play on the patio or on the grass," Mom answered.

She told me in later years, "When you entered the house and started walking around, my hands were just inches from your shoulders or hair for the first few minutes. I so much wanted to be touching you, but I was afraid of overwhelming you so soon."

My new mom and dad escorted me around the house. That gave me a chance to look more carefully at them, too. Mom seemed warm, happy, and excited to see me. She was larger than some of the "moms" I had had before, but not too heavy.

The Ryans were older than the foster parents I'd had. That didn't bother me; it actually made me feel more secure. But

44 *Please, Somebody Love Me!*

perhaps that age perception caused me to ask Dad that day, "How old are you?"

"I'm eighty years old," he answered with a straight face. He kept up that teasing joke for a long time.

Many years later, in a vocabulary test on the use of words in sentences, I described Dad. Some of the phrases were: "He is a very godly, formidable kind of man. . . . My father is not a loud man. . . . When entering or leaving a room he has a quiet manner. . . . He is a polished and neat man. . . . He has taught me well through his strict discipline."

But on that first day in my permanent adoptive home, my mind was more excited about the things I saw.

Mother took my hand and led me into my bedroom. There were dolls and teddy bears all over the bed, which was covered with a pretty pink bedspread. In the corner was a desk with lots of crayons, pencils, and paper. Everything was mine. I had never had such a room before. I didn't know what to think. What a difference from one foster home, where they had put me in a closet for playing with the other children's dolls.

When mother set down the few things I brought she said, "Jill, you'll never have to move again. You're home!"

Dad and I shot baskets out in the paved alley by our garage. The neighbor kids were expecting me. After school they came over; we chased each other all over the yard and up and down the alley.

Mom came out and found me hot and sweaty. To cool me off, she walked and I skated to the ice-cream store for a double-decker cone. Back outside, I lurched on my skates. Plop! went the ice-cream scoops on the sidewalk. It amazed me that Mom took me right back in and bought me two more scoops.

Soon my new eighteen-year-old brother, Mike, came home from high school. He had lots of red hair, liked cars, and worked at the supermarket. Perhaps it was the eleven-year age difference and the fact that he was busy with work, girlfriends, and college that never gave us a chance to form a close brother-sister relationship. Within five years he was married and gone from home.

Mom and Dad heard me up early one morning soon after I first arrived. They were still in bed but called me into their room and said, "Crawl up on the bed with us." I lay down between them and looked all around their room. Dad noticed me looking at the pictures of a girl on their dresser. He explained, with difficulty, that she was their daughter Becky. She had died when she was eleven, and they had loved her very much. He said that both she and Mike were also adopted.

I don't remember all he said, but he let me know they were happy to have me and would love me just as they did her. Though I didn't realize it then, his gentle explanation helped me begin to feel secure. Mom and Dad were careful to mention Becky in my presence only rarely and not to compare us. However, I had some of the same schoolteachers and Sunday school teachers she had, and perhaps they unknowingly gave me the impression Becky was an angel. I sometimes wondered if I could measure up to her standard.

My forever home was like no other I'd been in. My new mom and dad took me to Sunday school, morning worship, evening services, clubs, choirs, and everything else at church. Though Dad was a minister, I didn't know him as a pastor, except later for one year at a church in Claremont, California. He worked for the National Association of Evangelicals when I joined the family.

Mom and Dad sent me to our church's Bethany Day School in Whittier, California, near La Habra. Sympathetic Christian teachers loved me and helped me learn.

One day a few months after coming to my new home, Dad came into my room. He sat by me on the edge of my bed and said, "Jill, do you know what it means to become a Christian . . . to accept Jesus as your friend and Savior?"

"Not really," I said.

Then he talked gently with me in children's words about sin, guilt, God's love, forgiveness, and a new beginning with Jesus. He prayed for me. Then I prayed, asking Jesus to come into my heart. Even with a child's understanding, my experience that day meant much to me. But I remember wondering in the back of my mind if this God would ever really love a little girl like me. Could this new family love me? The old "rules" of being a foster child had been deeply instilled. Surely I didn't deserve their love. I was unworthy.

My spiritual growth would be slow. Over the years, as I changed physically, old emotional scars kept getting ripped open, delaying progress. Nevertheless, something was begun in me that day that, many years later, would bring me unbelievable joy and fulfillment.

One morning after I had spent a year with the Ryans, my mother called to me as I came through the door from school. (We were living in Claremont, California, then.)

"Jill, come into the sewing room." I would often find her there in the afternoon when I'd come home. "I have some exciting news for you."

"I'll see Mrs. Schlesinger again?" I cried in shock when Mom told me. "Oh Mom, when?"

That was how I learned that she, along with Dad's and Mom's social worker, would be having lunch with us before our day in court. Was I ever proud to host Mrs. Schlesinger in my own home! I even dared to ask her if she was a Christian. Both workers were ready officially to recommend the adoption.

Every year we sent a family Christmas letter to all our friends. Here's how Dad described me in our letter, just after the legal adoption:

> Now a precocious (in some ways) almost ten-year-old, Jill keeps the household alive. Laughter and tears, storm and calm, frowns and coy winks, words of fury and words of love, scraggly hair and sophisticated styling, earnest Bible questions and silly chatter alternate from this fiery but oh-so-warm and loving charmer.
>
> Quite uninhibited now, she will do a ballet dance or sing a solo (on key) for her class, or teach them an art lesson, or write and direct a skit, or play the piano for slumber-party singing.
>
> Last summer was her first eligible year at church camp.

Forest Home's Indian Village, where seven girls and a counselor sleep in each teepee, was just made for her. Habitually leaving or losing everything, she surprised the family by bringing every item home. More amazingly, she won the award for best camper!

It wouldn't do to omit the fact that in May the family assembled in a judge's chambers in Los Angeles for the final adoption decree. For better, for worse, for her and for us—Jill is a Ryan. She is not our adopted daughter. She is our daughter—period! That's the way it was from the start.

My parents tell me of times during this period when they laughed at my questions or comments. Once when Dad was tucking me in bed, I touched his dry, rough hands and asked, "Do you have whiskers on your hands, too?"

I was also fascinated with the many books in Dad's library. I saw one titled, *The Stork Is Dead*. My comment was, "poor thing!" (*The Stork Is Dead* was a 1960s sex-education book for teenagers.)

Yes, there were lots of fun times with my family in the early years after my adoption: visits to Disneyland, Knotts Berry Farm, Magic Mountain, excursions to the beach or the mountains; birthday parties. I especially remember the long car trips we'd take when we sang camp songs and gospel choruses.

But my years of misery could not be erased just by an adoption ceremony. I was still living by a lot of the old "rules," and hurt and anger still boiled inside me.

I found that it is one thing to need love . . .

    to want it desperately . . .

    to cry for it . . .

but quite another thing to *accept* love when it is offered.

I remember that during those years Dad would come into my room at bedtime to tuck me in, read a Bible story, pray, and say good night. But when he leaned over to kiss me on the cheek I would block him. That hurt Dad, of course, but he would be patient with me.

When I did let him kiss me and he had shut the door, I

would lie there crying softly, wiping off his kiss, unable to accept his love and affection.

My inner pain often showed itself in the form of behavior problems. Many times I threatened to leave home, even as a preteen. Once I asked to go back to the Martins, my last foster home. Maybe I was mad at my parents and wanted to hurt them.

One evening at bedtime I slipped out of the house and wandered around the yard in the dark. Mom found me missing when she went to my room to check on me. She came outside and finally found me crouched behind some big bushes. If I'd known there were huge spiders in those bushes I'd have surrendered a lot sooner.

Another night I ran over to my girlfriend Jan's house without my parents' knowledge and Jan's baby-sitter let me stay. It was eleven o'clock before Jan's parents came home, found me hiding in a closet, and took me home.

While we lived in Claremont, my mother worked part-time at a fabric shop a few blocks from our house. My baby-sitter took me for a walk to some nearby stores, where we stopped to browse. A clerk at a small department store saw me back up to a counter and scoop some costume jewelry into my back pocket.

The manager called the police and they called my mother. The policeman didn't put handcuffs on me or take me off to jail. But this eleven-year-old girl was scared he might do it. When mother told the manager that this was my first offense, he let me go with these stern words: "Don't ever come back in my store again!" But shoplifting was a problem I would have to work hard to overcome.

This was another signal to my parents that I would need outside professional counseling. They always provided any necessary or recommended help during my years at home.

I was on the edge of being a teenager. We were ready to move to Portland, Oregon, where Dad would open a new regional office for World Vision. And all the agonies and sorrows of my childhood were about to be magnified a hun-

5

How Can I Love Them?

"We love because he first loved us." 1 John 4:19

Greaser! Mex!

Two brothers down the street from our house threw those names at me every day on the bus that took me to junior high school. My unusual features—olive skin, dark hair and eyes in the midst of mostly northern European blonds—said "Mexican" to them. Also, the fact that I had moved to Oregon from the Los Angeles area reinforced their misconceptions.

It hadn't been this way at first. We'd become friends quickly when we moved into our beautiful new home in Portland. I was excited when the neighbor kids involved me in street games. Unfortunately, the boys didn't like my competitive attitude in sports. When I hit the ball farther and ran faster than they did, it may have been wiser not to let them see my satisfaction. They took it personally and soon plotted revenge.

One morning my family woke up to find the outside of our home splattered with eggs. My parents didn't accept this as the so-called fun of adolescence and called the police. When I was asked who might have done such a thing, I said, "Try the Brill boys down the street." My parents called their parents. When the boys heard about this, a war started between us kids that seemed to have no end.

Those boys received no discipline at home—their father was very uncooperative with my parents. In fact, my parents' complaining to the Brills only aggravated the situation. When they reached high school, the boys were what we used to call hoods—the ones who smoked, drank, and went to wild parties. I became afraid of them and their friends.

Once again, as in my earlier childhood, I became trapped inside my own fear. Afraid to fight back, I retreated instead, giving them more opportunity to win the battle they had invented in their minds.

One day after school their gang got off at my bus stop. Trying not to look afraid, I held my head up and walked confidently down the street. Soon a large rock smashed against my head. I ran home with a huge knot on my temple that turned black and blue.

The harassment escalated. It followed me into the classroom . . . the halls . . . football games . . . movies . . . wherever I went. The Brill boys enlisted other kids. From junior high through my senior year of high school, the harassment diminished, but it never left me.

At one point the Brills spread a vulgar "dog food" story. They called me "dog food." Kids yelled it . . . threw it . . . in the halls, at the games, on the bus. School leaders were never able to stop it. Deep humiliation crushed me. I withdrew from many social contacts because of what I was sure others were thinking and saying.

My counselor suggested I change high schools and confirmed this with the principal. Mom quit her job teaching sewing at a fabric store and faithfully drove me to another school several miles away for three years. But the Brill brothers and their friends passed their taunts on to people in my new school.

Even years later, on graduation night, the first question I asked my parents after the ceremonies was, "Did you hear any bad words or jeers when I walked across the stage?" I just knew there would be. But they didn't hear any comment. It was finally over.

Bad . . . useless . . . worthless . . . friendless . . . were feelings that seared my already battered self-esteem. The results in my teens and early twenties were monstrous.

Questions ate like acid in my stomach.

"What's wrong with me? Am I really such a bad person? Why can't I be loved and liked?"

Even at church, someone had a hard time loving and accepting me. One morning shortly after we moved to Portland, a woman who was teaching my Sunday school class stopped my dad on the steps after the worship service. The usual junior high schooler's hyperactivity, exaggerated by my emotional problems, bothered her.

"I don't understand your daughter. She disturbs my class. Her behavior is terrible. What's wrong with her? Hasn't she had enough discipline? She should be a better example for the class."

I don't know all she said, but Dad got the message that in her mind he and Mom had flunked the parent's test. Certainly no daughter of one who was in Christian work should act like I did. Christian friends, too, can be judgmental and low in compassionate understanding.

My parents didn't tell her I was adopted and had lived with them only the last five years. Even if they had, like most people she wouldn't know that five years—or a lifetime—can't fully repair damage done in those tender first eight years.

Later a well-known businessman, Bob Farrell, of Farrell's Ice Cream stores, was my teacher. He had the patience and love to hang in there with me. He would give me bear hugs or slip me tickets for sundaes at one of his stores. I still count him my friend and think of him with appreciation.

Somehow, through the years, no matter whether I was walking with the Lord or not, I was almost always in Sunday school and church. My parents never forced me, just expected me to go. I'm glad I did.

The nine years I lived in Portland weren't all in the pits, though sometimes it seemed that way. My grades in "core subjects" were never great. However, by focusing on my strengths of drama and music, I was able to be an achiever and gain the admiration I desperately needed. I also found a release for the painful emotions that surged through me.

In my junior-high-school orchestra I held first chair in the flute section and danced and sang my first solo in the musical "Nights in White Satin." I was doing what I liked to do best.

High school brought leading roles in *Inherit the Wind, The Sound of Music, Dracula,* and many other dramas and musicals. I also collected awards from intramural speech contests and became the district champion in dramatic speech.

I've always been blessed with a great ability to memorize. Mother always marveled at the telephone directory in my head. I could reel off almost any phone number with ease, whether we called that number often or rarely. That ability to memorize enabled me to master a role in a play, a dramatic speech, or words to a song quickly and recall them long afterward. That helped me make professional-quality presentations in any of those fields.

We owned a TV with an early-model remote control. It more than filled my hand and was about the size of a large microphone. When I was about fifteen years old, I used to pretend it was a mike. For hours at a time I would stay downstairs in the family/TV area of our split-entry home. Dreaming I was Barbra Streisand, I practiced her songs with that remote control, moved around my stage, and took my bows.

Mom and Dad always attended the plays and concerts I was in, and Mom sewed costumes or whatever else I needed. (She's an excellent seamstress.) I loved the patterns and fabrics I got to pick out for myself—especially a leopard print split-skirt corduroy suit.

Music was also part of my church life during my junior-high and high-school years. My first solo came one Sunday evening when I was a ninth grader. I was calm and ready; my parents shook with a major case of nervous jitters. But I pulled it off, and Dad and Mother lived through it. This opportunity was really a gift of confidence from our church's music staff that began to encourage my dream in the music field.

Between my sophomore and junior years in high school, my home church (Temple Baptist in Portland, Oregon) gave me a scholarship to the annual Christian Artists Music Seminar at Estes Park, Colorado. Linda, a friend from church, went with me. I wasn't ready to be serious about the classes, but meeting the artists whose names were known across America truly impressed me. The week helped me dream big dreams.

Dad and I, along with another passenger, stood in the elevator in his office building. The woman said to me, "You're a very attractive young lady. You ought to try modeling. I own the modeling school around the corner from the building. You should enroll—you have real possibilities."

Though I didn't take that woman up on attending her school, the idea of modeling rooted and grew. Until then, as a sixteen-year-old, I had dressed mostly in jeans, T-shirts, and athletic shoes. (I was active in sports.) But the fact that someone saw modeling potential in me helped my self-esteem and changed my dress from athletic to fashion styles.

Encouragement also came from a family across the street from us. Kellie Svihla became a close girlfriend when I had a hard time making friends in high school. We went through boyfriend experiences together, and she has always stuck by me. Even today, when I go home, I always see Kellie and the family.

I thought that Kellie's mother, Pat, was one of the prettiest women I knew. She always dressed beautifully and wore her makeup well. Her example also helped inspire me to go into modeling and to change my image from sportswear to pretty dresses and carefully styled hair.

Modeling schools teach not only how to model clothes, but also how to walk gracefully, maintain poise, keep up with styles, use cosmetics correctly, set a table properly, and other social graces. So my folks made it possible for me to begin attending the John Robert Powers School of Modeling in Portland when I was a junior in high school.

Active sports kept me in good shape during those teen years and served as another emotional outlet. In junior high school, I won first place in the decathlon and received the Physical Fitness Award signed by President Nixon. During high school, my folks twice sent me to a summer week of basketball/volleyball camp at Biola College in La Mirada, California. I played varsity volleyball and some basketball in high school. In track I was a fast sprinter and even did one season of football cheerleading.

Joy and intense pain often flowed at the same time during those turbulent teenage years. The brutal lessons of my childhood, added to the normal upsets of adolescence and my naturally high-strung temperament, combined to make life difficult not only for me, but for the ones I loved. We did have plenty of good times. But deep down, I hated myself and I repeatedly dragged my family with me through the dark caves of my mind and soul.

So often my anger at anything, everything, and anyone boiled over and scalded my parents. They never knew—and I certainly didn't know—why or what would trigger the anger. Normal teenage turbulence was a deadly hurricane in me. Even today my mind can't remember much of those teen years. My parents have to fill in those places where God mercifully allowed the memory of my extreme pain to be erased.

Dad did some traveling in his work, so Mom often took the brunt of my outbursts. Twice I threw heavy objects at her that landed on her feet, requiring trips to the hospital for X-rays.

56   *Please, Somebody Love Me!*

Another time I used the phone handset as a weapon against Dad. I whammed him just above his left wrist. He suffered no break, but the phone's plastic case cracked.

One time I finally said, "I don't want to live with this family any more!" And this time they took me up on my threat. They called county social services to explore the possibilities of my leaving. The social worker who visited explained: "If Jill is to leave this home, you will have to sign a release, so that we can take her until we determine what will be in her best interest. We could place her in a foster home. Before that, though, we will place her in a group home."

"Jill," she told me, "You will be living in a care center with two or three other girls. Special arrangements will be made for your schooling. You will remain in the care center except for school time. You will receive an allowance of ten dollars a month from the county."

That got to me. My parents had been giving me ten dollars a *week! "The county allowance wouldn't buy much of anything,"* I thought.

But although the idea of having less money bothered me, the words that really caught my attention were "foster home." That dreaded phrase cooled the whole idea of leaving. Maybe living with my family wasn't so bad after all.

"I . . . I'll . . . try to get along." I squeezed the words out. "I'll stay here."

Looking back, I can understand a little more clearly what went on that day. I had challenged my parents' discipline once too often. Dad was a minister, conservative in his reactions and decisions. It was important to him and Mom that I learn to behave well. But no matter how strict or conservative Mom and Dad may have been, they always showed unconditional love for me. Even in calling social services, they were trying to avoid making mistakes with me and to help me.

Today I shiver to think . . . except for teenaged greed and childhood fear (and surely, also, the grace of God), I could have lost my forever home!

Why
(written at age seventeen)

Who am I?
Why am I here?
Is life to love
Or a thing to fear?

What use am I?
What good can I do?
Were you my friend
Or just someone I knew?

What is love?
I really don't know.
Is it just there,
Or does it grow?

Why am I happy?
Why do I cry?
Why am I living?
When will I die?

Please, Somebody Love Me!

6

Bittersweet

"Who shall separate us from the love of Christ?"
Romans 8:35

The heckling and harassing I went through at school kept bruising old bruises and slashing old scars until I was now helplessly confused. I didn't care if I lived any more. The warning of my California counselor was coming true. She had said, "Jill will need lots of counseling when she becomes a teenager." The details of what were both tough and tender times during school years confirm she was right.

During all my turmoil, my parents were there, doing all they could to help me:

loving me . . .
    praying for me . . .
    hoping my church ties would help . . .
    providing professional counseling.

This morning I was a fifteen-year-old high-school freshman looking for help in the vice principal's office. I felt like I wasn't fitting in at school. I had stayed overnight at a girlfriend's house and gone directly to classes. Wordless sobs kept coming out for a long time. How could I say what I felt? I didn't even know.

The vice principal called Mom, and she called Dad.

This couldn't have happened at a worse time for Dad. He was scheduled to leave the next day on a trip that would take him around the world in a month. Many appointments had been set up for him.

But now his daughter needed help urgently. And immediately he put his preparations on hold to take care of me. First, he called a neurologist we knew, who referred him to another physician. That doctor arranged for me to be admitted as an inpatient at a Portland hospital. These arrangements would allow Dad's insurance to cover most of the counseling and ensure that I'd have the best help available.

In the early afternoon, Mom packed my suitcase, and Mom and Dad came to school to get me. According to them I left quietly, too upset to argue. When I asked where we were going, they answered, "To see a doctor." Even when we arrived at the hospital and I saw my suitcase, I didn't try to run away.

I asked Mom how long I'd be there. She said, "As long as the doctor thinks you need to be." But he had already told Dad I would stay about thirty days.

For all of us, as bad as things seemed to be, God was still in control and the timing was best. My time in the hospital really helped me, although sometimes I chafed at the confinement. Mom came to see me every day, and Dad sent me letters and cards from all over the world.

After a couple of weeks, two other girls and I managed to get out of the hospital and run away. The next afternoon, the three of us were out on the highway leading to the coast from Beaverton. I had told them we could hitchhike our way to Coos Bay, where my grandmother would let us stay. We stood there in the light rain with cars whizzing by. Finally, one slowed as it came toward us—a police car.

After we had been detained several hours at the county police office, someone from the hospital picked us up. The only harm any of us suffered from our adventure was that I got infected ear lobes—all of us had pierced our ears with the same dirty sewing needle!

I was released from the hospital in time to meet Dad at the airport. I didn't know whether to laugh or be embarrassed when he got off the plane wearing a round, decorated, native hat he had bought in West Africa. But we were all happy to be together and headed for home.

I always benefited from good counseling. The help I received while Dad was gone enabled me to handle the present and to begin to resolve the past.

In my life, as with life in general, I found that mixed with the bad times were good times . . . the unpleasant and the pleasant . . . the sad and the happy . . . the bitter and the sweet. But for me, the contrasts were especially intense.

Dad's influence has always been strong in my life and I have felt close to him. But like most children, I spent more actual time with Mom. Though I learned to be quite open and frank with Dad, there are some things where only a mother's understanding will help.

Besides time at home, we had time together when she drove me to and from school and other appointments for many years in Portland. When Dad traveled, Mom and I had our own dates out together. That was our chance to head for the fast-food restaurants—Kentucky Fried Chicken® and all the rest. But my favorite was always Taco Bell®. Mexican and other more highly spiced foods always gave me a zesty appetite.

If Dad was gone on a Saturday, I'd say to Mom, "Let's go to the farm today," and she'd come back with, "Get your room cleaned, the vacuuming done, and your other jobs finished first." Then we'd head out to my uncle's ten-acre farm about twenty-five miles away. I loved to see the horses or to ride the burros. My uncle raised calves for the market. It was fun to watch them bounce around the pasture.

Sometimes we went shopping together, but that was frustrating for Mom. Her ideas of appropriate styles for teenagers were quite different from mine. And she always wanted to sew for me. But I equated homemade clothes, even tailored by an expert seamstress, with being for the poor—what a foster child might have to wear. And I was desperate to make sure that image never clung to me. With a few exceptions, like the leopard-skin corduroy, I insisted on "store-bought."

Two years after the hospital experience, between my junior and senior years of high school, many people in my church shared in supporting my first Christian music witness outside my home church.

Having auditioned the year before, I was now accepted for a place in the Continental Singers—about a dozen choir and orchestra groups that travel each summer to different parts of the world. My group of thirty-five made a ten-week tour of the United States and then flew to Bermuda for six concerts. All groups finished their tour in Los Angeles at the Shrine Auditorium with all 350 voices praising the Lord before about six thousand people.

Close quarters in the bus and staying in private homes taught me many things about human relations, although I know that my emotional ups and downs sometimes caused distress for my patient director, Jim Chaffee, and my fellow travelers.

While the bus rolled along over the miles, I had time to think . . . to gaze out the window . . . to dream . . . to write my thoughts.

My Little Window

Hey, lonely girl, where are you going?
You look so sad,
Don't you know it's showing?

Why are you running,
Who are you running from?
When you look out your window,
Can't you see how far you've come?
I guess you can't, because
You've been running for so long.
You're so weak and tired,
Too tired to sing your song.
What happened to that little girl
Who wanted to be loved,
And then when it came,
She flew away like a dove?
Now look up into the sky,
Tell me what you see.
You can accept his love,
It doesn't cost—it's free.
He'll take care of all of you—
All your cares and dreams.
He'll take care of all your worries,
It's not as bad as it seems.
As I watched her closely,
I saw her slowing down.
I think she might try
This new love she has found.

(written at age seventeen)

The drive to know my roots was always there. I didn't look like anyone in my home. Who was I really? In both junior high and high school, I wrote papers on adoption, explaining how I wanted to find my birth mother. I even won a poetry contest for "Mama, Can You Hear Me?"

When I was ten years old, Dad let me play with his old reel-to-reel tape recorder. It became my friend as I told it my thoughts and feelings. Recently Dad located a tape I made and was able to have it transferred to a cassette so we could hear it for the first time in twenty years.

Over and over during the few weeks I made it, I kept reciting a list of the many different homes I had lived in—

the people's names, what they were like, and some of the abuse I suffered. How desperate I was even then to make some sense out of my life—to discover or remember where I came from, to trace my roots. I knew of no one person who could tell me where I'd been or what had happened to me during those years.

The first answer to my questions came suddenly one afternoon during my junior year of high school.

Sometimes Dad and Mom would have a special present for me. They would say, "Come into the living room; we have a surprise for you." Once it was the gift of my own stereo. This time it was a letter:

Dear Mr. and Mrs. Ryan,

My name is Jon Wallace. I live in Southern California. My folks helped me write a letter to the agency where they adopted me. I had a sister named Jill. She was adopted by someone else. They say you adopted her.

The agency told me that if I sent this letter to them they would forward it to you. I want to see my sister again. My dad says it's okay with them. He says it won't make any difference if we meet. I'm eighteen and Jill will be soon. The choice will be up to us.

Please write to the agency and give me your answer.

Sincerely, Jon Wallace

Silent images from my painful childhood flashed before me—especially my separation from Jon and those lonely times of matching hands through the car window. My heart beat double-time as I wondered, "Could this really be my brother?" It was the impossible come true. I was thrilled, but sad memory-tears flowed during much of that day.

Many times, as I grew up, when people had learned my name was Jill, they'd say: "Hi Jill! Where's Jack?" They meant it as a funny, friendly greeting. But each time it shot needles into my heart, for I knew I did have a brother somewhere.

I could think of nothing else for days after Jon's letter arrived. It came just a couple of months before one of the

Please, Somebody Love Me!

summer basketball camps on Biola's campus. I would be in Southern California then, and we could meet. Letters flew back and forth between us, and plans were made. The camp always held a banquet for parents of the campers at the end of the week. My parents were not able to make the trip this time, so Jon's parents were to sit in for them.

I played hard and did my best during the camp week, but Jon was always on my mind. When the day of the banquet arrived, we were still in our campus dorm rooms getting ready. Jon came up and stood by my door. The fact that he had olive skin, dark eyes, and rather sharp features didn't trigger any response on my part at first. I went in and out several times before he recognized me.

What screams of delight! Tears and an exchange of hugs delayed me and drew excited attention from the other girls. These were our first moments since we matched hands on the car window many years before.

Finally I met Jon's adoptive parents in the dining room. We felt a little awkward at first, but soon we were all talking. I learned that Jon had attended high school at a military academy. The rugged training there had helped him become muscular and strong. He planned to go into the army in a few weeks.

The Wallaces took us to their home in San Diego after the dinner. I stayed a couple of days so Jon and I could get reacquainted. I soon learned he didn't get along with his parents; that's why they had sent him off to military school. I also learned there was still a big gap separating us.

One day, while Jon was driving me around San Diego, he stopped at a bar.

"Jon, why are you stopping here?" I asked.

"Oh, just so you can meet some guys I know," he answered.

It was obvious that Jon's ideas of right and wrong were not what I had learned. I asked him to take me home, but he kept stalling while we argued. It wasn't a pleasant scene.

Jon disappeared when it was time for the Wallaces to take me to the airport the next day. They apologized when he couldn't be found; they thought my brother should at least say good-bye. Maybe he decided our meeting hadn't been such a good thing—we had talked a lot during that week, but we hadn't really "clicked." Or maybe he couldn't bear another separation and good-bye.

Whatever happened, I didn't see Jon again until he was out of the army three years later.

But I had touched and talked with my blood brother. At least I knew someone out there who was related to me.

High school days were almost over. In January, before my June graduation, someone gave me information on the Miss Oregon-Universe contest. My parents were less than eager for me to enter it, but I did. So on 27 January, after passing two days of preliminary interviews and appearances, I was one of the participants present at the Portland Airport Sheraton for the final events.

Although my parents were as supportive of me as they could be, I sensed they were a little uncomfortable and embarrassed that evening. For one thing, they felt the evening gown and the swim suit were inappropriate for a girl my age. But it was mainly because they knew I didn't have my life together. The experience helped me to be aware of that too, yet just trying gave me some satisfaction.

I dated a few boys from other high schools, but not from my own. I did become good friends with a boy at my school. Jeff and I met during our sophomore year. He was the only one who really looked out for my interests for the next three years. During our senior year, after our favorite late-morning psychology class, we'd go out to lunch and talk and dream about what we would be some day.

Jeff was one guy who treated me as a friend and had confidence in me. At the traditional yearbook signing he wrote, "Dear Jill. I really enjoyed our times together. You're a very beautiful girl, and I know you'll be a successful model some day. I'll see you when we're both famous."

The summer before my senior year, as every summer, I

Please, Somebody Love Me!

attended Lake Retreat, a youth camp near Seattle owned by the churches in our Conference. That year I met Craig, the boy of my dreams, who lived in Seattle. We hit it off and quickly became friends. The last night of camp, during a service, he reached over and took my hand. The whole world seemed to stop for the moment.

We dated throughout my senior year of high school. Though we lived three hours apart, we didn't let the distance separate us. Craig and another guy would drive the two hundred miles to Portland, and my parents would let them stay in our guest room. Sometimes I went to Seattle to visit a girlfriend, and I would get to see him.

When it came prom time, my friend Jeff and I wanted to be together. So Craig and my Seattle girlfriend, Cindi, came for the event and we double dated . . . Craig with me and Jeff with Cindi. Our psychology teacher provided a stretch limousine for us that night.

Finally the year was over and we all went our separate ways. Craig was my first romance and Jeff my good friend. When I think back I remember those happy days with special fondness.

One of the biggest surprises and greatest rewards of my life came when I was voted "most talented" by the senior class. It was in the yearbook for all to see. In spite of my inner struggles, and though I dated no guys in my own school and so often had fights rather than friendships with the girls, the recognition came.

The most popular girl in school had also been nominated for "most talented"—yet I was chosen. Why? It was beyond my understanding. Where did the votes come from? It could only be one thing: I had friends I didn't realize were there!

Bittersweet really describes those days in or out of school.

Chasing a dream of unknown existence,
Chasing a fantasy that passed by my way,
Chasing a horizon full of love and laughter—
But when I turn the corner, it's just another day.

7

Perverted Love

"Love does not delight in evil. . . . It always protects."
1 Corinthians 13:6–7

The evening began as a pleasant date with Chris—a Theater Ballet at Portland State University. A cold, mid-January rain greeted us after the performance.

Chris was not a Christian, but he pretended to become one and was even baptized at our church. He didn't want me to go away to college.

Outside of his effort to control me, I didn't see any problems at first. When I mentioned to my parents that he sometimes squeezed my arms, they thought I meant playful boy-girl acts.

I hesitated at the edge of the covered walkway after that January ballet. Other men were dashing to their cars to bring a coat or the car for their date. I was without sweater or jacket.

I asked, "Would you please get my coat for me, Chris?"

Without warning, a horrible, hate-filled look I had seen glimpses of before covered his face.

"You're coming with me," he growled.

With that he grabbed my arm, squeezing it unmercifully, and began to drag me along. I swung my purse at him, scattering the contents on the street. He let me pick some of my things out of the water as he kept dragging me to the car—publicly humiliating me. My only thought was, "Won't someone help me?" But no one did.

Once we were in his pickup truck, Chris alternated between total silence and loud, abusive words as we drove in the general direction of my home.

"But Chris," I kept protesting, "I just want to be treated like a lady." I hadn't demanded anything, just asked for some protection from the rain—something the other men were providing their dates.

"You aren't good enough to be treated like a lady," he yelled back. "You're just a worthless, no good————!" Foul words exploded, one after another.

When we came near Westmoreland Park, he slowed down and swung into a paved area under some trees. And then began a time of physical and emotional abuse a thousand times harder than all that had ever tortured my body and soul during foster years. Until long after midnight, Chris pounded out his hate on me.

I knew something of Chris's hatred for women, especially his mother. She had cheated on his dad countless times while his dad was away in the Navy, and Chris had watched her. Now I felt the wild fury of his anger, the horrible pain inflicted by muscles grown powerful from training for the Olympics as a gymnast.

Fists pounded my body. Cowboy boots stomped on me as he shoved me to the floor of the truck cab. Strong fingers ripped one side of my dress into shreds and threads.

With his explosions of wrath I heard every kind of degrading word he could think of.

He grabbed me by the throat, kept shaking me violently, smashed my head against the door again and again. I fought

70   *Please, Somebody Love Me!*

unconsciousness. When occasional cars came by—including a police car—I frantically reached for the horn, but he blocked the way and beat me harder than ever.

My screams—from pain and the hope that someone might hear me—soon became raspy whispers as he kept choking me. Even in my battered state—I wondered if I'd ever have a singing voice again.

When his anger finally played out, he threw me against the cab door once more and started the engine. I collapsed in a moaning heap. When he stopped in front of my house, he reached across the seat, opened the door, and shoved me out. I was exhausted, ashamed, and even felt some of my self-hatred telling me that I deserved what happened. So I didn't wake my parents in the early hours of Sunday.

I was usually the first one up on Sunday so I could get my shower, fix my hair, and do all I had to do before Mom wanted to use the bathroom we shared. This morning, when she didn't hear activity, Mother got up to see why. A quick glance told her I wasn't in the bathroom. Then she knocked gently on my door and called my name. I couldn't answer, so she opened the door.

"You'll miss breakfast. Aren't you going to Sunday school?"

When I tried to answer, she asked, "What's the matter with your voice?"

I told her, "Go look on the bathroom floor." She found my new rhinestone-trimmed white silk dress ripped from under one armpit down to the hem and covered with grease and dirt.

In hoarse whispers that came from somewhere inside me I tried to answer her question, "What happened?"

"He beat me . . . he beat me . . . I screamed for two hours while he beat me!"

Dad jumped out of bed when Mom ran to tell him. They both listened in shock to the few words I could get out. Mom pulled up a chair right beside my bed and sat with me for most of the morning. Dad made an appointment to talk to our pastor Dr. Fred Prinzing, early at church. He let the Sunday school class he taught know there was a problem at home, stayed with them for a short teaching time, and came back to the house.

Since I had no broken bones and wasn't bleeding, we didn't see a doctor or go to the hospital. But my angry parents wanted to stop this relationship and make Chris answer for his actions. Dad called a local judge we knew for advice on what to do. In a couple of hours, when I could begin to move around, Dad acted on the judge's advice and took me downtown to the police station to enter a complaint.

Dad helped me tell the officer what had happened. While the complaint was being drawn up, the officer had the police photographer take lots of pictures. Bruises were beginning to appear all over my thighs, forearms, and upper arms.

Then I did the unthinkable. I refused to sign the complaint. They gave us the pictures, and we left for home.

I know now that there was no sense to my refusal, no logic, no reasonable explanation—not even fear could account for it. How could a woman react this way? But I also know that battered wives and battered dates do it routinely—sucked into a living hell by perverted love.

My refusal to sign the complaint was a sick choice, just like many others I made during my three years living at home after high school. True, there were some good choices and good results, yet they were always mixed with the outrageously bad.

Immediately after high-school graduation, the summer before I met Chris, I worked at a health spa and at other jobs. It was always easy for me to get work. No matter where I've been or where I've wanted to work, I could go in and sell myself as the one they were looking for.

At home we talked about college, voice lessons, drama school, or other possibilities for that fall. Other kids from our church had taken a year of Bible training offered by Ecola Hall on the Oregon coast. It was a one-year course for people who didn't know for sure what they wanted to do, but wanted solid grounding in their faith.

Lori, one of my friends at church, had taken the training a couple of years before. She was three or four years older than I. Her excellent home background enabled her to reach out and invest time in me. We would go bicycling and take a lunch to eat in the park, or go out for ice cream, or play on the church women's softball team. She spent time with me every Saturday afternoon, discipling me as we studied the Bible together. That helped me make the decision to go to Ecola, which pleased my parents.

My earnings and the help of my folks made that year at gorgeous Cannon Beach possible. I listened to famous Bible teachers brought in from all over the United States and felt the encouragement of students and administrators. But my actions and reactions, fed by roots of bitterness and pain, disturbed others—especially the administrators. I couldn't follow the rules for on-campus living and even left campus against orders. Here, as everywhere, my inner turmoil often upset my self-control.

My pattern at Bible school, as in so much of my life, was usually two steps forward and one step back—sometimes one step forward and two steps back. But I learned. I grew spiritually. And I was much more ready to take a try at college by the end of the year.

Just before I came home from Ecola, my brother, Jon, phoned Mom from the East Coast.

"I'm back from Germany," he announced. "I got my discharge papers yesterday."

"What are you going to do?" Mom asked.

"I'm coming to Portland. In fact, I've already bought my air ticket. I'd like to store my stuff in your garage and stay with you for a while," he explained.

"But why aren't you going to your folks' place in San Diego? They'll want to see you."

"Oh, Mom is sick and Dad says I can't come home. Besides, I want to be near Jill and go to college in Portland."

We learned later that Jon's parents felt they had done all they could and weren't able to handle having him around.

Since Dad was out of town at the time, Mom made the decision to let Jon come. He stayed at our house for three weeks—until Dad told him he would have to start paying room and board. Then he got a job and moved out.

During the months that followed, with Jon living in the area, I really got to know him. And I realized it would not work for me to spend any more time with him. As rough as my life had been, God had given me a new one. And he had also given me a desire to serve him, even though I buried that desire so much of the time.

Though Jon's experiences were different from mine, he was a victim of his own circumstances. But in his battle to work through the destructive things in his life he didn't turn to God. Once again I was faced with the devastating loss of a male figure I needed to cling to—particularly at this time in my life.

Jon was my brother. Surely I could depend on him to save me . . . to teach me. After all, we were related by blood. But no . . . like Bobby in that long-ago foster home, Jon could not be a brother to me. Finally we parted ways, with a loss to me far greater than I had known. After two or three times together, I did not see him again.

Even in my school grades I experienced the bitter legacy of my early years. The adoption agency's psychologist had written these words as part of his evaluation just before my sixth birthday:

"Jill is seen as an extremely appealing youngster. Outwardly, she is self-possessed, outgoing, and friendly. . . . There is some tension in the learning areas. She is verbal and quick, but sometimes loses concentration and her knowledge is temporarily frozen."

Yes, "knowledge that was temporarily frozen," was a pattern that showed in school—my battle for emotional survival often interfering with the subject at hand.

I made application to several Christian colleges, but my

74   *Please, Somebody Love Me!*

poor grades in the high-school core subjects closed doors. Providentially, Seattle Pacific College in Seattle, Washington, agreed to open their doors to me.

During the summer after Ecola, I again worked and saved enough money so that with grants, loans, and help from my parents I could pay my way for college. One of my jobs was at the local Marriott Hotel, serving as a hostess in one of their restaurants. It was the year Mount St. Helens exploded in a volcanic eruption. President Carter was in the area to survey the damage and was a guest at the hotel.

As I was getting off work one evening, I saw a group of men walking down the stairway that led to the lobby. In the middle was the president. I dashed to the stairs, crowded past Secret Service men along the railing side, and caught him. I grabbed his hand and said as I shook it, "I'm a Christian, too!" He looked at me and gave me his famous grin. The Secret-Service didn't give the president full protection that night—at least not from me. It's a good thing I wasn't Squeaky Fromme! But that's how I've done everything in life. When I want something, I go after it with all my heart.

By the end of summer I was ready to go off to college in Seattle. My life's desire and dream that motivated me in high school drove me in college also. I was the only freshman to gain a leading role in the school play. I didn't do as well in other classes as I might have, but I succeeded in my areas of strength: drama and music.

By now, however, Chris was in my life. He would drive from Portland to Seattle on some weekends, and I would see him when I was home for holidays. Gradually, he convinced me that I loved him.

It wasn't that boys at college didn't look my way. One even sent a dozen long-stemmed roses to me at my home one weekend. I was ecstatic. No one had done that before. But I still believed Chris was the man for me.

Though I wouldn't admit it in a letter to my dad, Chris was helping change my mind about college. This is what I wrote:

Dear Dad,

Thanks for your letter! It really meant a lot to me. In replying I thought I would send this to your office address so that I could make it a little more personal.

I like it here, Dad. I see a lot of good reasons for me to be here and then other reasons why I would like to continue elsewhere.

I realize that you have gone out of your way for me. I think you have done that since the first day I was adopted. Now that I'm older and more mature, I look back and appreciate everything you and Mother have done for me. It has been *hard*—very hard—for me, spiritually, mentally, and physically.

I realize that my being here was very much a surprise to us and also a step ahead for me in my life. . . . Here are some of the things I've been feeling and that have been happening:

I feel frustrated a lot of the time because I'm not an easy person to get along with. It's easier to notice in a dorm-type situation living with other girls twenty-four hours a day. I have friends—don't get me wrong—but all I'm saying is that it's easier for me to see here exactly what I lack in communicating with others. . . .

All my life, as you already know, I have wanted to be in the theater and sing. First of all, for theater I'm definitely in the wrong school. . . . I know if I am to be a career-oriented person I will have to get training besides music and theater and work while I'm at it. Example: Take cosmetology (makeup) and theater and music. Then, after I get my license, I can use my talent on the side—in ministry or whatever. (This was my first time to use the word about myself or even think of ministry.)

Well, as you can see, these are the excuses I've found to come home and go to school somewhere cheaper and get more detailed training for what I want to do. . . . I don't want to make any decisions, though, until we have a chance to talk. . . .

I do not want Chris to have anything to do with my decision on returning or not. (Who was I fooling?) You know

Please, Somebody Love Me!

how emotional I get. Sometimes it's hard for me to make good decisions! That's why I have told you everything, so that you can help me make a reasonable decision when the time comes.

It's hard because I do miss my family, Chris, church, and friends, but I still want the best future for me. I appreciate your concern also and think of it as an act of love on your part. I love you, Dad, very much and I promise you one thing—that the man I marry I will definitely love and respect as much as I do you. Thank you for your support. See you Friday.

Love, Jill

I came home for Christmas and applied for admission at Portland State University on my twentieth birthday. Dad wasn't very happy with my decision, but he was always my friend.

One evening after Christmas he took me out for a delicatessen sandwich and cake at the locally popular Rose's. Then we attended the Portland Civic Theater's production of *Oliver!* The next day we drove to Seattle and back, bringing all my things home from college.

Dad and I went to a state championship football game, where a special friend of mine was playing. We saw stage plays together and often had lunch out. Our favorite place was the Bush Garden Japanese restaurant near his office. Sometimes when Dad wasn't traveling or having a business lunch, he would call me in the morning and invite me to join him. There were private screened-in rooms at the Bush Garden where we would eat, drink tea, and do our talking.

We also had other times to talk. I was used to talking with social workers and counselors. So sometimes when he would be in his study at home I'd knock on his door. When I opened it, he would pretend we had arranged a counseling session and invite me to sit down in the easy chair by his desk. Then he'd tilt back in his big desk chair, put his hands behind his head, and say, "Well, what shall we talk about today, Jill?" And I'd take it from there.

Yet less than thirty days after I enrolled at Portland State and Dad and I had that good evening out to see *Oliver!* I was being battered in the truck at Westmoreland Park.

It would be over a year before I could break away from Chris's insane and dangerous influence.

Changes
(written during the time of Chris)

Changes . . . we watch as they come
And we still watch as they slowly pass by.
Changes . . . something I could never understand
And I still find myself asking why.

Yesterday we met and time brought us love,
But tomorrow brought only tears . . .
One minute making plans and the next we
Break them—changes . . . that's something I fear.

Minute to minute, day to day—
Even hours never promise a thing.
Unexpectedly everything changes;
You never know what tomorrow will bring.

Changes . . . the things which happen
In between—the hurt, the sadness,
The pain of saying good-bye,
Of something you can't repeat.

So how can I believe you when you say
You love me? Maybe tomorrow you'll change
Your mind?
It's hard to trust you when it's hard
To believe—even when the things you say
Are kind.

8

Perverted Love,
Part Two

"Love is kind." 1 Corinthians 13:4

Chris and I argued and struggled in front of my church late one Wednesday evening. He was squeezing my arm and yanking me toward his truck. I tried to pull away. The Wednesday evening activities were over, and my family and almost everybody else had gone home. But one family saw us and wondered if something was wrong.

"Would you like us to take you home, Jill?" Mr. Sigley shouted from up the street where they were parked.

"No," I yelled back. I didn't want to go with Chris, but I also didn't want the embarrassment of their involvement. They drove away, and Chris finally got me into the pickup. Unknown to me then, the Sigley's had driven around the block and seen him pull me into the truck and leave.

This was happening only ten days after my beating in

Westmoreland Park. I had foolishly talked to Chris on the phone a couple of times during those days and seen him once. He knew he could control me. Part of the control came from the times he was nice to me. After the beating, for example, he sent me flowers. These and other gifts were always part of the persuasion to stay with him. One part of him gave me the attention I craved; the other part of him brutalized me and convinced me I was an unworthy person, deserving such treatment.

The phone rang while Mom and Dad were getting ready for bed. It was the Sigleys calling, terribly upset, yet not knowing whether to believe what their eyes had seen or how serious it really was. But Dad knew. He threw his clothes back on and sped the nine miles back to church, hoping we might just be parked or be driving around nearby.

As he went out the door, Dad said to Mom, "Call Carolyn [a neighbor and friend from church] and have her come over so you won't be alone. Put on a pot of coffee." It was about eleven o'clock when he arrived back at the church. He circled several blocks and didn't find us.

Dad then drove to a gas station two blocks from the church and called the police. When the patrol car met him there they scoffed at his story of my being forced into a car. Since I knew Chris, they assumed I must have gone with him willingly.

When they learned Chris lived in county, not city territory, however, they arranged for two county sheriff's cars to meet Dad on Southeast 82nd Avenue. After convincing them of the danger I was in, he followed them to Chris's house where Dad thought we might be. The officers, a man and a woman, carefully walked around the house and then began knocking on the door. No answer. They banged hard on both the doors and windows yelling, "Police!" Dad stayed in the street.

After several minutes, Chris decided we'd better answer the door or he'd be in trouble. He opened it and told me to talk. But no one could see that he kept a tight grip on my arm. One of the officers asked,

"Do you need help? Are you being held against your will?"

"No," I lied. I was afraid of Chris, but I was also protect-

Please, Somebody Love Me!

ing him—afraid of what might happen to him. It was a classic case of what today is called a codependency.

Then I snarled at Dad in a loud, hate-filled voice, "Why don't you leave me alone? Why don't you mind your own business?"

Dad's entry in his journal describes the next moment:

> At that, the officers just turned and slowly walked away. I was left in my embarrassment. Jill's response was just what they had predicted. Though we went through a lot of hurt with Jill, that moment stung the most. I knew then that there was little hope for her apart from a total miracle in her life. It was a very helpless feeling.

Dad got home after midnight but Carolyn was still there with Mom. They talked and prayed for me in those early morning hours. Carolyn was my friend, too. Though she had her own teenagers, she often took me out for pie and coffee so we could talk. When I was in junior high school, she had given me a bound book of blank pages. It became a book of my poems, through which I expressed feelings I couldn't share with anyone else. It was natural that she would be with my folks that night. As usual after the beatings I received from Chris, I eventually found my way home.

All through that spring I yo-yoed back and forth between being in Chris's evil grip and being free to do my college work and live a normal life. Dad told me that if Chris even stopped his car in our driveway or in front of the house, he would call the police. But I still saw him on and off.

In midsummer, Chris sneaked into an evening church service by slinking low down an aisle after church had begun and slipping into the pew beside me. But Mom and Dad saw him from across the sanctuary.

When the service ended, Dad rushed out ahead of anyone—up his aisle, across the lobby, down our aisle, to stand directly behind us while we were still seated in the pew.

First he grabbed Chris's hair, then shook his shoulders from behind and growled at him, "You're a coward! You're a coward!" Dad repeated this over and over. People around us were on their way out the pews and aisles. Surprise, question marks, shock were on their faces. No one said or did anything.

"You're a coward, a coward," Dad kept saying.

"What are you talking about?" Chris asked weakly.

"You beat women! You beat women! You're a coward!" The words kept flying back and forth. Dad spoke loudly and firmly. He was as angry as I've ever known him to be.

"Come outside with me, I want to talk to you!" Dad said as he pulled on Chris's shirt. Finally, Chris followed Dad out of the church to the front steps. The senior pastor had been the only one in the vestibule, standing ready to greet people, when Dad ran through to reach Chris earlier. He had seen Dad's anger. So when the two went out to the steps, the senior pastor sent a church staff member out to observe what was happening.

"You're psychologically sick!"

"How do you know? Do you have training?" argued Chris.

"Yes, I have. And I want you to stay away from Jill! Stay away from our house! Stop driving by and throwing rocks at the house to get Jill's attention." After a few other words Dad walked away from him.

I stayed inside . . . terribly embarrassed, afraid for Chris, not knowing what was happening between the two. I hid in the church. My parents searched but couldn't find me. Finally, they went on home.

In my emotional state, I did what was typical of my dis torted thinking at that time. After everyone was gone, I left the church, ran over to the bus stop at the shopping center, and took a bus to Chris's house. I was afraid Dad had beat him up—that he would need me—ignoring the fact that Dad was past sixty and certainly not in shape to fight! .

The sad fact was, I just couldn't free myself from Chris. The beatings continued.

It was during this time that I gave up completely. I was ready for the last choice. I even wrote out my resignation from life:

Please, Somebody Love Me!

Daddy—

I'm *so sorry*, Daddy—I tried *so* hard. Please believe me. I just couldn't do it any more.

I wanted to make you proud. I wanted to be everything that would have made you happy. I guess I wasn't strong enough.

I'm going home now, Daddy, and I just want you to know that you were more special to me than anything in the world. It killed me to keep hurting you, because I love you so much.

Daddy, remember the poem I wrote to you? I still cry from reading it because every word is so true. Please don't be mad. I had to do this because I couldn't go on any more.

I got lost along the way and just couldn't get right. I love you Daddy. I'll be waiting for you. I'll be there to greet you.

Please don't blame Chris. It was me. I love him. Say goodbye to Mom. I love you *both*. Thank you for my life!

Jill

Suicide seemed to be my only way out, but for some reason I didn't act. Mom and Dad didn't see the note until much later.

Two months after that awful scene at church, I came into the living room where my mother was and told her, "Mom, I want to go back to the hospital."

I was depressed, confused, captive to Chris. I knew that my parents' health insurance would cover day-to-day counseling only if I was hospitalized. I knew this was the only way. But I would be able to leave the hospital for my job at a cosmetics store.

When she called the doctor, he agreed to make arrangements for me to be admitted. But even during this stay, I would leave and see Chris.

While away from the hospital one afternoon, I met an unusually interesting young man named Stephen. He was both handsome and a fully committed Christian. He liked to stop by my store, and soon he wanted to date me.

Even when I explained to him about the hospital, he seemed to want to reach out to me. He began daily visits at the hospital to read Scripture and pray with me. With his guitar accompaniment, we sang songs and shared about Jesus with the others.

On one visit he brought a poem he had written for me. He believed in me, encouraged me, and said he knew God was going to use me in a great way some day. We dated a lot for a short time after my release, but I broke off the relationship. I felt I didn't deserve the love of such a fine man.

Many years later I was back in my hometown. He read in the paper of my homecoming concert and the celebration of the release of my first album, which was to be held at a huge church nearby. That evening he brought his wife and children to the concert. How I wept when I saw his smiling face, met his family, and heard these words, "I knew you could do it."

His poem reminds me today how God used an ordinary person who was willing to take a risk—to dare loving someone who was confused. It also reminds me of other good relationships I so easily passed by because I could not love myself.

From this time on, our pastor, Dr. Prinzing, began to suggest to me that it might be a good idea if I moved away, perhaps back to California, and make a completely new start. And I started to think he was right.

It was during these months of late summer that I met David. He was so different from Chris—so gentle, so kind, never sexually aggressive. He treated me the way I wanted to be treated—like a queen. He told me how pretty I was and often complimented me on my clothes. Chris never did that. "Surely this must be my knight in shining armor," I thought.

Occasionally, during that fall, when I worked evenings at a cosmetics store in the Clackamas Town Center (a large mall), David and his friends would walk me to my car so Chris wouldn't bother me. Chris began to realize that, with David in my life, he really could lose out.

Christmastime was beautiful at the Town Center. I loved the decorations and the crowds, and I loved my job, selling cosmetics.

One evening, just before the nine o'clock closing time, Chris came into the shop. Over the last few weeks he had been begging me to come back to him. This time he forced me out of the one-clerk store. I stumbled and protested as he squeezed me with his powerful hands and walked me through the crowded mall, out to the parking lot, and into his pickup.

"I've got to close up! I've got to close up the store!" I kept telling him. "At least let me get my coat," I begged. But he wouldn't listen or let me go. Somehow I sensed that he was ready to do almost anything. He followed the shopping traffic out onto Sunnyside Road and to I-205. All the time he alternated between threatening me and begging me to come back to him.

He turned off the freeway and drove slowly up the dark, lonely road to Mount Scott that leads past two cemeteries. A road leading into the middle of one of them was open, so he turned in. Then he stopped, shoved me out of his pickup, and drove away.

I struggled to my feet as the pickup's taillights disappeared. The December cold immediately penetrated my thin dress. But I don't know whether the cold or my horrible fear made me shiver more. Chris knew what he was doing—nothing could frighten me more than being abandoned in a cemetery at night.

Unknown to me, back at the cosmetic shop my knight in shining armor and a girlfriend of mine had come to escort me. They saw my abduction from a distance. And although they hadn't wanted to confront him there and cause a fight, they had followed us—first out to the parking lot, then, in David's car, to the cemetery. When they saw Chris's pickup speed off, they turned in to the cemetery and rescued me.

Of course I lost my job, because I had been unable to close the store. What had promised to be a happy Christmastime had turned into a nightmare. Chris had won again.

But that experience made me think seriously about leaving Portland. My regular counselor, Angie, told me: "Jill, Chris is sick beyond cure. The next time he gets physical with you, he could kill you! If you don't stop seeing him—and perhaps even leave the area—that really could happen."

Years later, I was astonished to learn that Dad had also been afraid that Chris would kill me. More than once, in despair, he had said that he would not be surprised to receive a phone call or a knock on the door telling him that my body had been found lying in a ditch beside some lonely road.

In spring of that year, I left for San Diego with David and my brother, Jon. It was my last time with him. I had only thirty dollars in my pocket.

For the next six years, San Diego became my home town. It was also where I became known as Jillian, a name I have kept ever since.

Taking the name of Jillian was part of my attempt to get rid of little Jill. All through school I had hidden my foster-child identity. I was embarrassed by the image of a poor, worthless waif who really didn't count for much and didn't belong to anyone. Perhaps my new name could stand for the new, successful person I wanted to be.

The name Jillian also has some logic behind it. Before I was adopted, I had no middle name. Mom and Dad had given biblical names to their other two children, so when they adopted me they gave me the middle name of Anna, who was a prophetess in Luke's story of Jesus' birth. Jill and Anna merge nicely into Jillian.

I always wanted my parents to think I was living with Christian women or families. That was actually true only about half the time. But there were some genuine Christian people who befriended me and helped me when I was down emotionally, financially, or spiritually. How grateful I am for them!

My first job was singing with a rock-and-roll combo. We did three or four concerts a week. But when I began to think about the Lord again, I felt I shouldn't be singing with that group, so I left it. Finances were tight.

David and I began attending a large, biblically sound church in the city. I sang in the choir and had a solo part in repeat performances during their Christmas festival. This church helped me with two months' rent and the deposit on an apartment when I had no place to go. Many individual families, too, were kind to me during my financial crunches.

In the spring I received a government loan to attend a school of cosmetology and become licensed for makeup and skin care. From this I was able later to move into doing "makeovers" for women and then to modeling clothing and fragrances.

My first full-time job as a cosmetician took me to Hilo, Hawaii, where I handled the skin-care department of a beauty salon. Once again, by being in a strong church and finding Christian friends, I was able to survive spiritually. But I wanted to be back in San Diego and to see David, so after a few months I left for the mainland.

David met me at the airport with a dozen roses and a ring. We spent a lot of time together, and six months later we married. But it wasn't a complete marriage. After the wedding I was totally frustrated. Why wouldn't he kiss me? Why didn't he touch me as a man should?

I thought, "Surely there's something wrong with me; I'm being punished for reasons I don't understand."

I was devastated when I discovered the real reason why my gentle, loving David was unable to be a husband to me. And although we tried to work out our problems, the painful finality became obvious that night back in Portland when I confronted him in the condo and later crashed my car on the bridge. David and I had no marriage—and no future.

I became angry later when I learned David had been in counseling with one of the staff at church for a year before our wedding. David should have been warned never to marry. But nobody had warned me that his problem was real and something that shouldn't be part of my life. In my bitterness I was sure I would never go into a church again.

I couldn't blame my parents. I was a thousand miles from home—and twenty-three years old. Dad and Mom did their best to support me and to keep the lines of communication open, but they didn't try to tell me what to do.

I really was the one planning out my future. And much of the time I had been living in a dream world, adjusting the facts to fit to my fantasy of a tender, kind, and thoughtful husband. I wanted to walk with the Lord. But, instead of submitting to God's plan, I was trying to make it on my own. I even thought I could manipulate God into giving me what I wanted.

I still needed a complete healing from my past. And like many experiences in life, that healing came as a serendipity. God brought me to it when I was looking for something else.

Show Me a Love

Is love a commitment—
A lifelong dream?
Does anyone know
What love seems to be . . . ?

When you say words like "I love you,"
When you wake up and they're on your mind,
You could spend every moment together,
And still not have enough time . . .

Show me a love—
Show me how to feel,
Show me what people call
A love that is real. . . .

If you should ever hurt me,
How could I go on?
Do I know how to forgive you,
And if I don't . . . is it wrong?

What if you break your promise,
Don't do the things you say?
What if you decide to leave?
Was love a temporary way
To have me for a moment—

Pretend that I was all yours,
Knowing you would never keep me?
What was love really for . . . ?

Show me a love—
Show me how to feel,
Show me what people call
Love that is real. . . .

Show me a love—
Show me how to feel.
Does anyone know
A love that is real . . . ?

9

Letting Love Inside

*"He heals the brokenhearted and
binds up their wounds." Psalm 147:3*

Once again I was trying to find my way out of a
bad situation and into recovery. After that final, brief inter-
lude in Portland with David, I was back in San Diego. I
plunged into modeling again to regain my self-respect by
looking good on the outside and making good money.

But at night, when the cameras and spotlight were turned
off, I'd go home . . . look in the mirror . . . take my makeup
off. And there she'd be—little Jill. I couldn't hide from her
any longer.

A year went by. Living alone gave me time to think. In a
long letter to Dad I expressed my thoughts and feelings:

I see a pattern I've made for myself with men in my life—
men I've chosen to date. For some strange reason, I seem to

91

punish myself through the men I choose. I let them do it for me. It must be a sign of what I feel I deserve in life. Or how I feel I should be treated as a person.

It seems that only in my dreams that I find that Special Someone who treats me like a lady and shows affection and loves me in the way Christ would. . . .

When . . . I look back on all the possibilities and potential I had, it breaks my heart to see how I used them and the pitiful mistakes I've made.

I'm so tired of mistakes! I'm so tired of heartache and regrets. But I'm going to learn from them. A tough lesson, isn't it? But I *am a survivor!*

Though I was by no means spiritually healthy, God was giving me some insight into myself and into my up-and-down relationship with him. Further on in the letter I shared some of my deeper yearnings:

I'm inspired to sing again—but I won't, of course, 'til I show some consistency in my walk with the Lord. I really believe the Lord is going to use me in a unique way once I get my life in order. . . .

I think it's about time I take spiritual inventory and clean out the closets and grow up! Enough of compromising my morals and living in the world.

I'm going to restore my life through the Lord's help. I'm going to be a godly woman with the Lord's help. And some day, Dad, I'm going to marry a man who loves the Lord and who will love me and treat me the way the apostle Paul talks about. I just want you to be part of my life, even though I'm not there. I want you to go on my walk with me—I need you to be proud of me and to encourage me. I need you!

I'll be thinking about you and Mom as you prepare to retire. I love you both and appreciate *all* you've done.

Obviously, at that point in my life, I had a yearning to live a life that would gain God's approval. You can't know Jesus as Savior, even following at a distance, without the Holy Spirit's prodding, rebuking, nurturing, and shaping your

Please, Somebody Love Me!

life. But truly yielding and knowing deep healing of my soul were yet ahead.

In the middle of that letter were some paragraphs about someone I'd met. Oh, I tried to convince Dad and myself that I wasn't on the rebound from my David experience. But I was. He was a handsome young professional with great potential for success in his field. Although he was only a nominal Christian, his family regularly attended a fine local church. Eighteen months after I wrote that letter there was another wedding ceremony.

The 125-mile stretch of the I-5 freeway between San Diego and Los Angeles became an all-too-familiar part of my life for many months. While modeling fragrances in the best stores in San Diego, I received a call offering me an opportunity to introduce the new Giorgio line in Beverly Hills. Sometimes I was provided housing in the best hotels and didn't have to make the drive more than a couple of times a week. It was a dazzling life, but that freeway drive also made it a wearing one.

Some might think that modeling fragrances is a simple job. But selection for such an opportunity is based on personality, attractiveness, and the ability to model high-fashion clothing, facial makeup, and the best jewelry all at the same time. My ability to sell myself by my appearance and personality made people want to buy the product. A few years earlier I made single cosmetic sales of as much as five hundred to a thousand dollars to wealthy women or Japanese businessmen searching for a gift.

While my work was an honest living, somehow I was becoming less satisfied with it. The lifestyle and outlook of the people with whom I associated became less appealing and incompatible with what I felt the Lord wanted from me.

One day the minister of music stopped me in the hall at church: "Do you know that Jerry Bernard's program on Trinity Broadcasting Network is running a contest looking for a gospel singer?"

"No! Tell me what I have to do!" He had my full attention. I had not been on TV before, but this might be my chance. What would I wear? What would I sing?

I didn't know there would be so much competition—more than fifty contestants. The actual contest was held in a large auditorium. I chose to sing "Because of Whose I Am," an excellent testimony song. It has a fairly wide range, but I picked it because it provided an opportunity to use my chest tones most effectively.

I was anxious the days before the contest and extremely nervous that day. But when the moment came to audition, my drama and music experience kicked in to give me poise and confidence. When I talked to one of the judges afterward, he used my favorite expression: "That was incredible!"

I came in second. Along with first and third place winners, I sang many more times on this nationwide cable program. Other TV opportunities soon came up, as well as invitations to sing in churches and for other groups.

During these months I finally acknowledged to myself that I was in another painful relationship. Things were desperately wrong in my marriage—things that could not only destroy my new effort to obey the Lord, but destroy me as a wife and person. A friend felt that the book *Help for Hurting Women,* by Florence Littauer, could help. It became a major turning point for me.

The book showed God's healing in the lives of several prominent women who had gone through unbelievably bad experiences including physical and sexual abuse, alcoholism, divorce, and more. Yet in each woman's story there was always the same conclusion—a time of emotional healing and forgiving others and themselves.

As I read *Help for Hurting Women,* the picture became clear to me. I had been running from the one true Answer too long. The Jesus I had accepted into my life as an eight-year-old was the same Jesus who gave these women healing, a new start, hope. I thought, "If Jesus mended their broken dreams, maybe he will do it for me."

A few weeks after reading that book, I heard about a major event to be held at the Anaheim Convention Center near Disneyland. Called "Praise '87," it was to present major Christian speakers from across the United States in a weekend event. Pat and Debbie Boone were the music headliners. But the program would also include a "Showcase" of young gospel singers to help the public become aware of them.

I responded to the invitation to send in a sample voice tape. On 5 March 1987 I received a full-page letter from Praise Ministries in San Bernardino. In part, this is what it said:

Dear Jillian:

One of the most exciting parts of the Showcase is that you will be a part of it! There were many applicants and the selection was a tough choice, but for many reasons you were selected and we are looking forward to having you with us for "Praise Celebration. . . ."

We are excited to have you on the team. We look forward to seeing you May 28–30 and are anxious to hear your fifteen-minute mini-concert.

Wildly and tearfully happy about the opportunity, I called everyone I knew and even told people I casually met.

However, it was the signature on the letter that really caught my attention: "Marita Littauer." Littauer isn't really a common name. Could this woman have something to do with the Littauer who wrote *Help for Hurting Women?*

Sure enough, when I made a telephone call I found that Marita is the daughter of Florence Littauer and that the Littauers were associated with the ministry sponsoring the event. Florence is a well-known speaker who has written many books especially for women. I soon met her and became friends with Marita. They helped me so much in learning how to develop my own music ministry. And they gave me hope for the future.

But more wonderful than anything else, they told me about their friend Lana Bateman of Dallas, Texas, and about her "Philippian Ministries." Lana trains spiritually and emotionally mature women in the United States, Canada, and Latin America to conduct "prayer days" for those who have suffered great emotional trauma. These are one-on-one prayer sessions for emotional healing that cover one or two days.

Arrangements were made for me to have my prayer day—my healing day—in Los Angeles with Lana's assistant, Angela. I was both fearful and hopeful as I drove that morning from San Diego to Los Angeles. But my inner need urged me on.

Angela's beautiful hillside home had a commanding view of the ocean. After greeting me graciously, my new prayer partner led me to a small, quiet room off the living area—something like a study—which she called her prayer room. There were just two chairs. It was a comfortable, intimate setting.

But I felt intimidated at first by this poised, mature woman and said immediately, "You strike me as a self-assured, self-sufficient person. Will you be able to understand my pain?"

"Yes, I will, Jillian. I have suffered too."

She took notes as I talked through my life and we prayed about each devastating experience. It was not a day without pain, not a day of vague prayers and requests. We sat across from each other, close enough to touch when I needed reassurance. I cried much of the day, and her tears flowed, too.

Before deep healing could take place I had to dredge up from my memory all the evil that had bruised and crushed me. Childhood abuse, the feeling of being abandoned, emotional starvation, physical wounds, word-wounds—all were relived. I felt again the rejection at school, the painful gouges of Chris's boots, the fear and loneliness of the cemetery, the anguish of failed relationships. I had to face my own repressed anger, my own bad choices, my rebellion against God.

And in the process, God became so real to me.

The toughest time of all was the forgiving. I needed to see

Please, Somebody Love Me!

the people who had hurt me not through my eyes, but through God's. If I was to be free of the past and of those hurtful people, I needed to forgive them. Otherwise my inner anger and hate would finish the destruction they had started in me.

Patiently, carefully, wisely, my prayer partner led me step-by-step to victory over every hateful memory. She helped me understand the spiritual battle and real enemy of our souls as described in Ephesians 6.

> Finally, be strong in the Lord and in his mighty power. . . . so that you can take your stand against the devil's schemes. For our struggle is not against flesh and blood, but against the . . . powers of this dark world and against the spiritual forces of evil in the heavenly realm (vv. 10–12).

It was for me a serious and complete surrender of my life to the Lord—a major turning point.

Since I had had helpful, therapeutic, professional counseling as needed through the years, this day before the Lord tied everything together. It brought fresh spiritual insight, a sense of my own forgiveness, and a forgiving attitude toward others. While no one experience could carry me through the rest of my life or make me immune to trouble, I could now begin to live a life of victory. I had really let love inside.

Sometimes, unfortunately, that kind of inner change can be threatening to people close to us. That happened to me. After my prayer day, the spiritual, emotional, and sometimes physical oppression that occurred during the first six months of my marriage not only continued but also increased. Still, I was determined to live a clean life for the Lord and to be obedient to him.

And while this determination brought opposition at home, it brought good things, too. Out of my own personal healing, for instance, I had something to share with others. I was no longer afraid to let people know me. All the way through school I had hidden the facts about my early life. I didn't want to be different, whether as a foster child or an adopted child. But now I found that I *wanted* to tell my story—so that I could tell about my wonderful healing as well.

I soon began singing again regularly. And when I sang, I would give a spoken message also and perform songs that reflected my personal experience. A concert ministry began to develop as pastors opened up entire evening services, or part of their morning services, for me to give my message. I sang and spoke to Navy groups, prisoners, schools and colleges, women's luncheons, ministers' meetings, and I gave radio and TV interviews. Exciting things were beginning to happen in my life.

One thing that many churches and other groups lack when having a guest concert artist is a good sound system—not just for speaking, but to handle music adequately. It was becoming more obvious to me all the time that if I was serious about my ministry, I needed a good sound system of my own. I made an appointment with Jim Neal, an executive I knew at World Vision headquarters in Monrovia, California. He had also given concerts in the past, and I felt he could help me choose the right system.

But I received more than the needed counsel on sound systems from Jim. I met with him and a man named Mike Motley. They said to me, "World Vision is again working with gospel artists who can give concerts and present our ministry. I think parts of your story could help people understand hurting children everywhere. Would you be able to travel with your concerts and present the Childcare sponsorship program of World Vision?"

"Is this really happening or am I dreaming?" I thought to myself. It had been only a few months before that I had been down on my knees and asking the Lord, "Can you, will you ever be able to, use me?"

Now tears came to my eyes as I looked at Jim and Mike and told them yes.

"But," I said, "coming from a modeling background I'll have to tone down my appearance."

They answered, "People will love you just as you are.

And your story will touch their hearts and help them identify with all children in need."

What a boost of confidence this new opportunity gave me! Going to churches, working with pastors, watching people's personal needs being met after I sing and speak, getting children sponsored for World Vision—all these things would bring me blessings.

I would not become a formal employee of World Vision, but would work with them on a contract arrangement to seek sponsors for children under their care. Thus I would become World Vision's national gospel artist, presenting concerts for them across America, in addition to continuing my personal concerts. In one year alone I would be able to gain nearly one thousand sponsors for children. My concerts would take me from California to Florida, New York, Minnesota, Washington state, Hawaii, and many other parts of the country.

But all that was still in the future when I called my parents in Portland to tell them of my new role.

"Hey, Mom, Dad, guess who I'm working for!"

"Don't keep us guessing! Who is it?"

"World Vision!" I nearly shouted.

After recovering from the shock, Dad said, "Congratulations. But what did you do? Who did you talk to?"

Some people assume, because Dad had worked for World Vision, that he made the arrangements. But he was retired and didn't even know about it. Nevertheless, working for the same organization where Dad worked for so many years has been wonderfully fulfilling for me.

When I first began singing in my teens and early twenties, I asked Dad to let me sing for the many banquets and other events his World Vision office put on for donors. But he knew I wasn't ready—certainly not ready spiritually. Now I did it without him, and he was proud of me.

Twice I was privileged to visit World Vision projects in Latin America. And during those visits, the needs I described to my audiences—the poor housing, the shortage of food, educational opportunities, and medical care—

became more than just words for me. They were people. I saw, touched, laughed, played, ate with those children and their families. Now I could talk to my audiences out of first-hand experience.

I also learned a personal lesson from those people in Ecuador and Costa Rica. I could see how I had spent so much time perfecting the outside of me, when for so many years I had little inside. These people, in their poverty, had little on the outside. But so many of them had so much on the inside.

Another encouraging experience came during those early days of singing for World Vision. I was asked to represent the organization and teach a seminar session at the Christian Artists Music Seminar at Estes Park, Colorado. I walked into the registration area for those in the music industry and saw a face that brought back memories from earlier years. It was Janice Chaffee. Her husband, Jim, had been my Continental Singers tour director when I was a teenager. He is now Executive Vice President of Christian Artists. Janice sat at the desk helping people register. I waited quietly. Janice looked up and said "Next." Then she slowly stood to her feet and said, "I know you."

I answered, "Yes, I think you do." When she asked me to help her remember, I simply said, "I'm Jill."

Janice almost screamed as she ran from behind the table and threw her arms around me, saying, "Oh, Jill, we always knew you'd make it. We've prayed for you. We wondered what happened to you . . . where you've been. It's so wonderful to see you."

Janice and Jim had had a tough job keeping me under control as a teenager on that tour. But they stand out in my memory as two of the people who helped me become a winner instead of a loser. Seeing Janice again was a wonderful confirmation that I was going in the right direction.

Once a person is involved in concerts as I was, sometimes four or five times a week, there is a demand for records and tapes. After talking to a number of producers, I was able to do a recording under the title *Let Love Inside*. Several thousand copies would satisfy the demand for a year or so, although I knew I could sing much better and needed a much improved sound track and total production.

With that album, however, I returned to Oregon for my "homecoming" and was featured in several newspaper articles. Then I presented my songs for the first time in concert at New Hope Community Church near Clackamas High School, where I had graduated. I was even invited back to school to give a program for drama and music students. After singing a few songs from my tape, I answered questions for twenty minutes.

As part of my story I told about singing with a rock band, but mentioned that I had to quit to sing in my music ministry. One boy asked, "Why couldn't you sing both kinds of music? Why did you quit the rock band?"

That gave me an opportunity to share briefly about my convictions and tell about the totally different lifestyle I felt God expected of me. Afterward, several of the girls who understood came to me and expressed their appreciation.

My husband wanted to take my life in a direction my conscience wouldn't allow. But once I had my inner healing day he was dealing with a new person. I could not, would not, allow him to use abuse in my past as a weapon to disparage me or allow him to degrade and abuse me in his own ways. But my newfound strength aggravated the tension between us even more.

For my own physical and emotional survival, I had to escape not only the home I helped purchase but also the city in which I lived, and begin again. I moved to Nashville. And I am so grateful for friends who stood by me; for my parents who sorrowed for me, yet understood; and for my friends, especially my boss at World Vision, who knew the facts and still believed in me.

Starting over financially, getting established among new friends, and maintaining my inner equilibrium were not

10

Can You
Love Me Now?

"May you live to see your children's children."
Psalm 128:6

Step back with me to a time not long before my day of prayer and emotional healing. It was a Thursday morning when I finally unlocked the door on little Jill. Can I ever forget that day? A girlfriend who was a fellow employee in San Diego and who was also adopted had told me about finding her birth parents. Though it wasn't pleasant for her, her experience started me on my own active search.

Five years earlier, when I was twenty-one, my parents had given me all the background information available on my birth family. Most important was the family's name, the specific place of my birth, and my birth father's occupation. But I had had no desire to act at that time.

This particular morning, however, I awoke with all kinds

of thoughts about my family of origin. Though I'd had contact with my brother, Jon, as a teenager and on brief occasions as a young adult, I still had loads of questions. And I still fantasized about my birth mother and what she looked like. Who was I like, and why did they give me up? I didn't look like anyone in my adoptive family. Was there someone out there somewhere, perhaps my birth mother, who looked like me? My hands shook as I picked up the phone and dialed the Los Angeles information operator. When I gave her the name "Bader," she told me she had three listings. I took all of them and called the first one.

It was impossible to hide my shaky voice and hesitant speech. An older woman, perhaps past sixty, answered.

I asked, "Is this the Bader residence?"

"Yes," came her strong reply.

I wasn't ready to reveal myself yet and gave her a fictitious name. I wasn't sure if I should break into their lives. Then, with my heart beating wildly, I asked, "Do you have anyone in your family who has ever been a professional in the beauty industry?"

"Why, yes, that's my son," she answered. I trembled as I realized I could be talking with my birth grandmother.

"Could you give me his number, please, or tell me how I might get in touch with him?" In my own mind I was sure he was my birth father.

She stalled me with, "No, I can't give out that information, but what I can do is have him call you."

I hadn't thought any further than this point, and I didn't know what to do. She took the false name I gave her, but my real phone number, and politely hung up.

What to do next? What kind of chain reaction was I setting off? I did what I usually did in tough situations—I called home.

Fortunately, both my parents were there. I explained what I'd just done. They were as excited and nervous as I was. We cried together. After some words of caution about what I might be getting into, they prayed with me on the phone, "Lord, if it is your will that Jill find her birth family, you can surely make it happen." They advised me to call back and give the woman my real name. Perhaps she would help me from there.

I could hardly dial that Bader number again, I was crying so much. When the woman answered, I managed to get these words out, "Mrs. Bader, my name is Jill."

There was a long pause—then weeping. She turned away from the phone and said, "Grampa, our little Jill has come home."

He picked up another phone and excitedly shouted, "Wherever you are, get on the first plane! I'll pay for your ticket!"

The Amtrak schedule for the one-hundred mile trip fitted best. That same evening I got off the train in the huge, old, Spanish-style station in Los Angeles. My grandparents were there to meet me. We spotted each other easily. Our similar skin tones, look-alike noses, and slim body frame helped me know Grampa at once. Tears, hugs, and animated conversation—with everyone talking at once—were a hopeless effort to bridge more than twenty-four years.

It was only a fifteen-minute drive to their hillside house. In the few hours that had gone by since my telephone call, they had organized a big celebration at their home. They had arranged for a beautiful "Welcome Home" cake and a lot of other refreshments.

There were aunts and uncles and cousins for me to meet. Flashbulbs popped all evening as we took group and individual portraits. Everyone possible was there but Jon, my mother, and my father. My mother had disappeared shortly after they separated, and no one knew where she was. My father, who had never remarried, had been practicing his profession for many years in a ski-resort town in another western state.

Later in the evening, Grampa put his arm around me and said,"I think it's time." He walked me over to the telephone and dialed my birth father's phone number.

"Josh, I have someone here you need to talk to." He handed the phone to me.

"Hello, is this Jill? I can't believe it's you." The shock of unbelief quavered in this male voice out of my past.

"I always hoped you'd find your grandparents some day."

Questions such as "Who were you raised by? Did you have a nice home?" followed one after another. Small talk and his comment, "I hope I can see you soon," mingled with my tears in closing our brief conversation.

In the years since that reunion, I have visited my grandparents many times, occasionally staying overnight. They even attended a concert I gave in the Los Angeles area. My adoptive parents have also visited them more than once. Dad got them to let him tape some of their life story and family background, which stretches to the East coast and across the Atlantic into Syria and Lebanon.

So I have more roots than I ever dreamed. You see, I have Syrian, French, Irish—plus some Native American blood from my mother's side. My grandfather prefers to use the identification of Lebanese rather than Syrian, because many of the Lebanese were Christian while the Syrians were predominantly Muslim. But the Arabic background is the same.

Not everyone recognizes my profile as Syrian immediately, but many do. Most people are instantly attracted to the striking features that combine in me. Dad was always impressed when I'd be dressed up and we'd walk to a restaurant in downtown Portland. In his side vision he'd watch both men's and women's heads swivel toward us.

It would be a year before I had a full visit with my birth father. He did stop in San Diego once, but I was sick at the time and saw him only briefly. I made repeated efforts to have time with him and was disappointed when his promised visits weren't fulfilled. I could only guess that he was ashamed of giving me up and didn't know how to deal with his guilt. That's one of the down sides of such family reunions. I didn't intend to hurt my birth father, but my very presence inevitably recalled the past and how he had handled it.

Finally, I decided that if he wasn't going to come to me, I would go to him. It was near Christmastime. I lined up three

106   *Please, Somebody Love Me!*

concerts in the area of his ski town and made arrangements to stay with him the week before. I wore my prettiest outfit on the plane. As I sat there, I realized that in a few moments I'd be talking to the father who had abandoned me twenty-four years before. What would happen? What would I say to this man?

The small-town airport, accustomed to hordes of celebrity ski buffs, was fairly quiet this evening and quickly cleared of passengers. I stood almost alone with my suitcase and waited. Once again that old videotape of long ago began to play in my mind.

I saw a little girl sitting on a couch in foster homes looking at the front door, and imagining . . . dreaming . . . wondering . . . hoping he would come—but he never did. Somehow I had imagined that if I was good enough, didn't get into trouble, did all the right things, someday my parents would be back for me. Now, standing alone in the little airport, the child in me asked, "Will he come now?"

A man walked toward me from the left side of the terminal. I knew he was comparatively young, but he looked aged. When he stood directly in front of me, he looked into my eyes and said,

"I know you're Jill . . . you look just like your mother, Mary."

I couldn't keep back the tears any longer. Josh and I had an incredible week together. There were dinners, walks, skiing, and shopping together. And there were many explanations, along with many tears.

At one of our dinners I told him, "I forgive you. In spite of, or because of, the experiences I've gone through, I can forgive you. Because of being in my adoptive home I have received and gained what I never could have had otherwise. Yes, I forgive you."

But the most dramatic and memorable moment came the night before I had to return home. I had just given a concert in a large Baptist church. It seemed as if the whole town had come out to celebrate our reunion.

After I had sung the last song, Josh stood up. Most of the

time he had been hunched over in tears. Two of his buddies sat with him, one on each side. Then Josh faced the congregation and said something that has touched my heart ever since, "If your God can take a two-year-old girl I remember leaving twenty-four years ago and make her what she is today, then I know your God can forgive me."

What a beautiful way to end that week together! We went to a restaurant afterward to snack and talk. He said to me, "I'm so proud to be your birth father! I can't get over your beautiful singing voice. I want you to know that God is more real to me right now than at any time in my life. I've asked God to forgive me for abandoning you and for not being your father."

As I say to audiences everywhere, don't we serve a God of grace and forgiveness and healing? He loves us no matter what we've done—no matter if someone has hurt us or we have hurt someone. We can be a victim of child abuse or have gone through divorce or any other trauma and still come to the place where we can forgive the people who did those things to us.

Two years after my visit with Josh in that mountain resort, I was going to be in a nearby city again. We had been in touch by phone several times since my visit. So I called him again, hoping I might stay with him between the two weekends when I had concerts. But there was no invitation. In fact, I received a rather sharp rejection. Then, a few days later, Josh called, apologized, and invited me to stay when I was in the area.

I was to be in his home for a full week. But the visit did not turn out at all the way I had hoped. Josh was forty-five minutes late in picking me up from the airport. And on many of the days that followed I'd wake up to find a polite note: "Jillian, I've gone up the mountain skiing—see you later." He would return many hours later, stumbling and reeking of alcohol.

It was such a letdown for me. I thought we had talked

through all this—that he really wanted me to come. He had told me he was proud of me and excited about building a new relationship. But when we were in public, he didn't introduce me as his daughter even once.

Before the week was over, Josh rushed into my room and said, "I need for you to go. You are too painful a reminder of my past." Somehow he was unable to fit me into his life at all. The memories I evoked were too tough for him to handle.

That ripped me apart. I arranged for an early flight out and hurriedly packed. Then I called a taxi and cried all the way to the airport. It was a terrible rejection.

I did learn a needed lesson, however. As the outbound plane sliced through the skies above the snow peaks, the Lord helped me understand that *I* cannot save Josh, but *God* can. I have to commit him to God, pray for him, and let my concern rest there.

Strangely enough, something else came out of that visit— a song. Before Josh asked me to leave, and realizing something of what was going on in him, I went up the mountain on the ski lift and waited in the lodge near the fireplace. I had hoped he would come in and we could talk. He didn't. But while there I began to write a song about his need and how God could fill it. On my album, *Defender*, it is called "Every Tear You Cry." It describes what God can do for anyone else, too.

Although some of my experiences with Josh were painful, I am thankful to have met my birth family on my father's side. Now I know who I look like. I understand why I have this olive skin, these brown eyes, these striking facial features. And other traits are obviously part of my genetic heritage as well. Without my knowing about Josh, for example, I entered the beauty industry, his occupational field. We both have an artistic flair and the temperament to go with it. He is extremely outgoing, as I am. And there are people on my paternal grandfather's side whose lifetime career has been in music. My birth mother also liked music and was a ballerina.

The grandparents I have met are loving, caring people who have accepted me completely. My picture had stayed on the dresser in their bedroom in the same house for nearly a quarter of a century. They had been terribly hurt that they were not allowed to keep my brother and me when their son's home broke apart, and all through the years they hoped I would find them someday. They loved me then. They do now. Knowing them has been a real gift in my life.

Today I have baby pictures from them that I had never seen before. I can see what I looked like from the beginning. Now I'm not so different. Just to see those people with whom I share flesh and blood was fulfilling. Being accepted by my grandparents and learning of their caring love has helped restore my self-esteem. I know I can't bring back the years I have lost with my birth family. I have no illusions about a fairy-tale ending to my search. But knowing where I came from helped me be at peace. I have roots. I have a birth family!

The Child in Me

Lord, I want to be the child in me
Free to run to your arms of love,
Free to do what others dream of.
Help me see what I want to be—
The child always living in me.

I want to dance
With my hands lifted high . . . .
I want to soar with wings in the sky,
Sit on a cloud, maybe read a book,
Race around the moon if that's what it took.

I want to feel what I've learned not to feel,
I want to love what I know is real,
I want to trust when others have quit trying
And not be afraid of where we go when we're dying . . . .
If only I could be the child in me.

Please, Somebody Love Me!

We've learned not to feel,
We've learned not to trust,
We've learned to pretend and do what we must
To get through each day our mechanical way
As our little child dies inside . . . .
Lord, I want to be the child in me.

11

Understanding Myself and Loving Others

"And this is my prayer: that your love may abound more and more in knowledge and depth of insight."
Philippians 1:9

The outside of his greeting card carried familiar words I'd read many times. But today, those words were more relevant to my life than ever. I felt a warm glow of love as I read once again the card Dad had timed to arrive in Nashville on a day he knew could be very difficult. That potentially lonely day would mark the final page in another chapter of my life. So now the beautiful words resonated in my mind:

> God, grant me the serenity to
> Accept the things I cannot change,
> The courage to change the things I can,
> And the wisdom to know the difference.

As I thought about those words on the outside of the card, I found a note on the inside which I will always treasure:

Dear Jillian,

Other than Scripture, the words on the front of this card have meant more to me than any others and have been my strength for many years. The last six words are the most important. May they in some way become wisdom for you.

I want you to know again how much I love you, and the great hope I have for your future . . . as a gospel singer, a counselor to abused women and children, and a voice for God.

You have so much potential within you. My prayer is that the Lord will make you a daily overcomer of every dark thought within and that he will be your shield from every poisoned arrow from without.

On this Monday, be with friends, go out to dinner, sing your favorite songs, read your favorite Scripture. And let this day launch you into the future God has for you.

With a hug and a kiss,

Your Dad

In just those few lines, Dad had managed to remind me once again that I was loved, that God's Word must be an active part of my life, and that it's important for me to do those things that bring me a positive feeling about myself— things such as singing, helping others, reading my Bible, and having relaxed time with friends.

At the bottom of the card, he added this powerful, life-changing Scripture to his note: "Forgetting what is behind and straining toward what is ahead, I press on. . . ." (Phil. 3:13–14).

Dad knew and understood the process God had put me through to make me whole again. He knew how Paul's words, written in the midst of his own personal struggles, could help keep me afloat when times were tough in my daily living.

For me, the first step toward healing and wholeness actually started with "forgetting what lies behind."

I had to forget.

But "forgetting" did not mean trying to block out a terrible memory. Instead, I had to work through the pain, with the forgiving love of Jesus Christ, to the point that I could put it behind me. And only God could help me do that.

Much of this "forgive and forget" time came with Angela, my prayer counselor, on my special prayer day. Together, we walked through each hurtful and tormenting experience.

"Now Jillian," she would say, "as we pray this time, I want you to lift up the anger and hate that began when you were a little girl, when that foster mother scarred your face by slamming you against the wall. Let those feelings take a shape—visualize them as looking like sticky, messy tar. Give that black, clinging mess to Jesus, who wants to take it from you. Can you do that?"

"Yes, yes," I replied. "I gladly hand that tarry pain over to him." As I did, it just disappeared.

"That's good," Angela said. "Now, can you ask God to forgive that harsh, abusive "mother" who inflicted both the physical and emotional pain? And can you forgive her, too?"

"I think so."

"Well, ask him out loud to do it."

"Lord," I began, "through your love, I forgive that woman who didn't know how to care for me. Maybe she didn't even realize how much her actions would damage me. Lord, in your name I forgive her."

With each hurtful memory and the persons involved, I did the same thing—other children, adults in my childhood, peers in my adult life.

As I spoke the words of forgiveness, tremendous feelings of breakthrough and relief permeated every part of me.

It's not easy to forgive someone who knowingly hurts us. But the process, no matter how hard it seems at the time, is a necessary one. If we don't get those memories out of our minds through God's forgiving love, they will simmer in our souls like a vile poison, polluting every healthy part of our being. Failure to forgive is ultimately self-destructive.

But it is important not only to forgive those who have hurt us, but to ask the people we have wronged to forgive as well. It's like taking a walk through our lives and stopping at each place of pain to forgive and shed excess baggage before moving on.

"Forgetting what is behind and straining toward what is ahead, I press on. . . ."

In forgiving others I have been able to understand myself more fully. I've combined those new insights with others I'd gained previously. Now I can see myself more as God sees me—a whole person—and life makes sense.

For instance, I have come to understand that a piece of paper with the word *adoption* written on it cannot erase nearly eight years of previous living, or their results. The "rules" I learned during those early years—unhealthy coping skills and thought patterns—brought effects that roared through my life like raging bulls. Certain survival skills appropriate for a damaged childhood produced exaggerated and distorted results in my early adult life.

For one thing, I was addicted to abuse. Remember Rule Five? "Sometimes abuse is good. Let them hit and hurt you. Then they'll feel sorry for you afterward, and you'll get some attention and treats."

The lead-in to tolerated abuse is low self-esteem. That came with Rule Three, "It's okay for people to do horrible things to you, because you're different from other people." And Rule Six, "Foster children are the same as animals."

A teenaged girl or young adult woman who has been abused in childhood can be a recognizable target for the male abuser. He senses her vulnerability by her low self-esteem. And, of course, he himself may have been abused also or witnessed abuse in his home. Abuse is a vicious cycle. Without God's healing and forgiveness, it's all but unstoppable.

People ask adult women who are victims of date or marital abuse why they don't just walk away when the attacks first start. Like many simple solutions, that doesn't fit reality.

As with most other women, my reasons for staying in abusive situations stemmed from faulty thought patterns that were rooted in my deep self-hate. Here's what would happen:

1. I would think, *It was really my fault. It's me. If I were a better person, he wouldn't treat me this way.*
2. I would believe him when he tearfully apologized and promised never to hurt me that way again. Then would follow a time of tender affection. He would tell me he needed me—and I desperately needed to be needed in order to feel worthwhile. Then it would all happen again.
3. If I showed any signs of breaking away, he would tell me I was worthless, unlovable—that no one else would do all the things he had done for me. And once again, I would believe him. Why not? I'd been telling myself the same thing for years.

And so the cycle of abuse repeats itself. Over and over, adult abuse victims replay what happened in their childhood, with results that are readily seen by family members and others as senseless, inappropriate, and self-destructive. Outsiders just don't understand why the victim responds the way she does or how the past has programmed her to make that response.

But thank God, I'm not trapped in that destructive cycle now! The Lord never let go of me even when I walked apart from him. When he knew I was ready to listen and respond, he provided my day of prayer and healing.

Since then, I have been able not only to minister joy to others in song, but to speak words of healing and encouragement to those in emotional pain.

About a year after my move to Nashville I was on a weekend concert tour in the Northeast. My Sunday evening concert in a big-city downtown church was over, and I was relaxing in the home of my hostess. An abuse counselor who had heard me tell my story at the concert called to ask if I would meet with a group of women at the church the next morning.

"These women have been meeting once a week for several months to encourage and support one another," she explained.

"Of course I'll meet with them," I gladly replied. Immediately I was filled with anticipation. I couldn't wait to see how God might use me and what he had in store for these women seeking help.

I returned to the church to meet the women on Monday morning. The night before, the church had been filled for the concert, and the evening was one of joy and praise. Today there was a much smaller group of people, all women, sitting in a circle. Not one was smiling. Instead, a slight look of embarrassment flashed across their faces. They seemed to be wondering if they would be able to share their most painful secrets.

"Good morning," I began after being introduced, and I started to tell my story as I would to any group who had not heard me before. "I'm Jillian. It was at the age of four that I realized I was very different from other children. . . ."

As I broke the ice by starting to share my own experiences of abuse, the unsmiling faces began to take on color and life. Our meeting became a beautiful session of mutual trust and shared backgrounds.

One woman I can't forget was a very attractive person named Sharon. I couldn't help wondering what she was doing there. During the early part of our session, she was very quiet, spending most of her time staring at the floor.

But then, as another woman was telling about a painful experience, a sudden burst of tears from Sharon startled both me and the group. After the initial explosion of pain shattered the quiet, I learned why Sharon had been meeting with this group of women.

When Sharon was very young, her father had begun a

Please, Somebody Love Me!

pattern of sexual abuse. It had started with taking baths together, then developed into molestation and finally incest.

I felt Sharon's agony as she released those pent-up emotions she had held inside so long. I fought unsuccessfully to hold back my own tears as she begged me to give her a way to forget such a painful, long-term experience—to really feel clean again.

I explained to her about forgiving and forgetting.

"But Jillian, why should I forgive him? He's an evil man who did vile things to me! How can I forgive him or forget what he did to me?"

"I understand how difficult that sounds," I answered. "If I hadn't forgiven my abusers, I wouldn't believe it was possible, either. But you must realize that your father is a product of this satanic, evil world in which we live. God gave us all the freedom to choose between right and wrong, between life and death—the freedom to know him through his son Jesus Christ. Unfortunately, you are the victim of your father's wrong choices."

As Sharon sobbed, I hugged her. Then I added: "You're left with the damage of your father's sin. But by the power of God, you can be a healthy, whole person again. That's what God wants for you. And that's what you want for yourself."

Sharon's pain was so real. She knew she desperately needed to forgive this man and to work through the bitterness she had buried deep inside.

"I don't see how I can do it," Sharon cried. "Jillian, how did you work through your hurts?"

"The way I worked through mine," I continued, "was by following the advice of my counselor. One of the things she suggested was that I go to a private place where I could think. I was to write down all the ways people had hurt me—every act . . . every face . . . every remembered agony.

"Then, I even prayed for a recall of memories so I could be sure to write down everything. You know, it's easy to bury hurts so deep that we're not even consciously aware of them. And it's natural that we don't want ever to pull them up again. But sometimes they pop out on their own when we least want or expect them."

Sharon nodded as though she understood what I was talking about.

Then I told her, "Once I felt my list was more or less complete, I prayed a prayer of forgiveness for those people who had hurt me . . . whether they asked for it or not! I reminded myself I was doing this because God had told me to—because it was necessary for my health—*not* because the other person deserved it.

"Another thing you can do after your list is made is to find a creative way to let it go. Maybe you went to summer camp as a child. At campfire time you wrote a wish or a commitment or a prayer and then joined others in dropping the papers in the fire. You can do that kind of thing at home at a stove or fireplace.

"You need to watch that list of hurts *visibly* go up in flames so you realize those memories are gone. Speak your prayer *audibly* as you ask God to help you forget. Hand those hurts and those people over to the Lord in prayer."

"Oh Jillian," Sharon said with her first smile breaking across her face, "that sounds like a beautiful idea."

As we hugged, I recognized the first signs of hope radiating from her eyes. I saw her excitement and sensed a determined desire to become a forgiver just as she has been forgiven by God and to become a healed person.

In helping another person find her way out of a painful past, I had another confirmation that I had found wholeness. For I realized that I now understood myself and was free to love others.

There is a realistic question that deserves an answer: "How does an abuse victim deal with memories that still reappear occasionally, even after she has exercised forgiveness?"

It does happen. Some unexpected event, some thoughtless person, or revisiting a certain city or neighborhood may release a ghost of the past.

One night after a concert in New York state, my own

screams shocked me out of a dream and awakened others in the home where I was staying. My bed was in the corner of the room, with a wall at the head and side. In the receding fog of my nightmare, I realized that the closeness of the two walls had put me back in that foster-home doghouse. Probably the rereading of this book manuscript while I was flying to the appointment stimulated the dream. It was one of those things a person can't anticipate. And when it happened, I had to give it to God once again.

Almost any day, unwelcome thoughts or fantasies from the past may surface. That's something that really never ends. The Bible warns us of another source outside ourselves—the accuser, the liar, the tempter commonly known as Satan. That deceiver doesn't stop his work just because we've experienced healing. But the difference for me now is that God enables me to exercise control when the thoughts come.

When I wake each morning, I consciously give my thought life over to the the Lord. As Paul said, "we take captive every thought to make it obedient to Christ" (2 Cor. 10:5). I've found I must work at developing a daily, hourly, habitual pattern to defeat old memories and unwelcome thoughts.

There will be times when unkind people say or do things to harm us. Or we may believe they intended harm because past abuse has conditioned us to think that way. We need to get the facts and correct them if it's necessary or possible. But then we can leave the results to God.

Most important is the necessity to be open in our lives—to be transparent, not hiding things. Then what do we need to fear from the past? "If God is for us, who can be against us?"

pieces together. He challenged my personal walk with the Lord and today is my best friend. We have the same church home and try to encourage each other spiritually. When I have a heavy tour schedule, especially when it includes large churches or other facilities, Mark accompanies me to handle the sound system and many other details.

One afternoon after a morning church concert, Mark suggested that something was missing in my concerts. At that time, I was beginning to speak more of my own personal testimony in the concerts. But Mark said, "Jillian, you're leaving people in tears. They're crowding the aisles to talk with you and bombarding you after the services—wanting to share their experience, asking for help, wanting to have prayer. But there's no response opportunity built into your concerts."

We decided right then to have an "altar time" as part of my concerts, if that was acceptable to the pastor of the church where the concert was held. People need to be able to respond—to express outwardly what is happening inside. Giving people an opportunity to come forward for a special time of prayer is an old custom in many churches. This can be the first step of faith in a new direction for their lives as they respond to the inner prompting of the Holy Spirit. It is a quiet time of prayer for them and all the congregation as those in need ask for healing of their emotional pain or help with any other area of their life.

Jesus said, "If you hold to my teaching, you are really my disciples. Then you will know the truth, and the truth will set you free" (John 8:31–32). At another time he said, "I am . . . the truth" (John 14:6). For those who recognize their need for emotional healing and want prayer, it's their moment of truth. They can call upon the One who is the Truth and the healer of all hurts. This is where recovery begins.

I look back on my prayer and emotional healing day in Angela's home as the point where I really let go of the garbage in my own life and began learning to love others. Now, after my concerts, I have the chance to reach out to people in their pain—right where they are, just as they are. I'm learning how to pray effectively with one whose child is dying, who is going through divorce, whose husband is leaving, or who is suffering abuse of any kind. The mental filing system of my own experiences helps me understand these people's needs, and my Bible studies and training help me speak what I feel will be the most helpful for their emotional healing. The time after my concerts often becomes just as important as the concert itself.

"Since I came to your first concert here a few months ago, my life hasn't been the same." Tears glistened in that highschool boy's eyes. He didn't open up further, and I didn't pry, but I'm grateful for those words.

Another time, a teenaged boy rushed up to me after a concert and clutched at me, not wanting me to get past him without hearing what he had to say. I'm glad I stopped to listen.

"I'm a foster child now, too," he blurted out.

"Well, hello, friend," I responded, recognizing his kindred feeling.

"My father was just put in jail for abusing my sister and me. My sis and I have been put in different foster homes, and I don't know if I'll ever see her again."

He could hardly control his tears and sobs as he told me what was happening in his life. I had no pat solution or magic formula, but I could show that I understood. And I could assure him that he and his sister were not alone and could, by God's grace, survive and compete in the world. I told him I would pray for him and encouraged him to talk to his youth counselors or those on the pastoral staff.

One time a woman whispered to me, "I pray for my daughter every day. She's a prostitute." People tell me all kinds of sorrows, revealing the ache in their hearts, even as that mother did.

On a different occasion a mother confided through her tears, "My daughter just gave up my two grandchildren for adoption, and I'm brokenhearted." People hurt, and they want to talk to someone they feel understands. There's an awesome power in a listening ear.

After a particularly tiring concert in Florida, the middleaged pastor came rushing up to me.

"Jillian," he began, puffing as though he had just run a mile to get to me, "I want you to know what's happening here tonight. A young couple was present who have been in counseling with me for three months. Frankly, they weren't making real progress. But they heard you speak about forgiveness, and now they are sitting in their car in the parking lot praying together. I believe that this very moment God is restoring their marriage."

Those words from the pastor refreshed my body and soul as I headed back to my hotel.

A woman sat at my table one day during a luncheon where I was providing the program. Before I could say anything, she started to weep. "Jillian, I've been such a horrible mother. I've abused my two little babies. I just couldn't control myself. The other day I voluntarily gave them up to foster homes. Can God ever forgive me?"

That woman sitting in front of me symbolized so many of the "mothers" who had hurt me. In a flash I was aware how God had wonderfully released me from my bitterness and anger towards all those "moms" and prepared me for this moment. In the past I had no tolerance for the abuser, only love for the abused. Now I felt nothing but compassion for this woman.

We talked about why Jesus came and what he wanted to do in her life. And I said, "Of course Christ can forgive you, just as he so freely forgave those who abused him when he was on the cross."

I was able to listen to this mother and help her without passing judgment on her for her actions. That was a victory in my life too!

Sometimes I receive encouraging letters that tell of positive steps taken by my hearers. A pastor's wife wrote, "You rekindled the spark of a neglected decision we made to care for a foster child."

Another letter said, "Your story gave us further confirmation that we should adopt this girl we have been considering."

126 *Please, Somebody Love Me!*

These are some of the blessings that keep me moving ahead. But there are hurts of others that leave me hurting for them.

At the prayer time after I sang and spoke at a church where two teenage girls were recovering from abuse, the older girl testified that her nightmares were becoming less frequent. I had talked that night about being forgiven but not being healed because of bad memories and low self-esteem. Realizing after my story that the span of time between nightmares was growing, she knew it was a positive indicator of God's healing of her torment. The story I learned later of this family's pain left no doubt in my mind that there would be nightmares.

It was the day before Thanksgiving, 1988. The pastor's phone rang. The caller was a distraught and agonizing father who gasped out, "Pastor, help me."

This man's two teenaged daughters had been living with their mother and stepfather in another state. And he had just learned from the authorities that the stepfather with the full knowledge of the mother, had been sexually abusing both girls.

The stepfather and mother were addicted to hardcore pornography, and the stepfather would act out with the daughters what he learned from the films. The stepfather and mother would then view the films with others and engage in group sex. This went on for more than eight years before the mother finally came to her senses and turned the stepfather in. Both were convicted. The mother is serving more than a seventy-five-year sentence. The stepfather received sentences totaling over a thousand years. The word *parole* will never be mentioned for him.

The girls' biological father brought the girls back home and asked the pastor to counsel with the girls. Knowing he was not qualified to meet their counseling needs, he began to build a trusting relationship with them so they could better express their feelings with professionally trained counselors. The girls have been in intensive counseling for two years; healing is slowly taking place.

What these girls and many other abused people need to know is that full healing after damage does not come with a snap of the fingers. Forgiving takes time. Working through memories takes time. There is a recovery period, and that's acceptable.

After a concert in a large church out West, a beautiful woman whose clothes said "wealth" approached and asked to talk with me. Then, she proceeded to tell me her story. Robyn's mother had died when she was a small child. Her father, a pastor, had molested her from the time she was eight years old until she was well into her teens.

Through her tears Robyn told me how her father would come to her room and require sexual favors in return for help with her homework or other things she needed. One time after this happened he looked upward and said, "If I do this again, strike me dead!" But a few nights later he was back with her. While he was molesting her, Robyn's eyes once caught a picture of Jesus on the wall. She could only think, "Why *don't* you strike him dead? Why don't you do it?"

That woman lived with her tormenting memories for years and kept wondering in bitterness why the Lord had never intervened and struck down her father. She felt dirty—never "good enough"—thinking all the time that she was destined to have bad things happen to her.

After our prayer time together, Robyn determined to go back and forgive her father. Now her faith and life are being restored.

Shortly after appearing on *The 700 Club's* "Heart To Heart" with Sheila Walsh, I was back in Nashville meeting with my manager. An urgent call came through—a staff person from the program requesting that I talk with a woman who had seen the show and called in, desperate to talk with me. I let the station patch me through.

I heard the trembling voice of a mother calling from the

hospital room of her fifteen-year-old daughter, Aimee. Aimee had recently been called as a witness at the trial of a leader in their church who had been abusing Aimee since she was twelve. When she learned that, despite her public humiliation, the man had simply been released, Aimee had plunged into depression. She could not go back to school— or any place.

One night while her mother was at work, Aimee had decided to end her life. She had taken over forty pills of lithium, a medication that had been prescribed for her intense depression. Incoherent when her mother found her, Aimee had been saved only by a fast trip to the hospital. Despite having her stomach pumped, Aimee had slipped into a coma, only to awaken three days later, the day of my telecast.

The mother had stayed close by in the hospital room and was flipping through the TV channels when she had come to the one where I was talking with Sheila Walsh. "Stop," Aimee had cried. After listening intently, she had looked at her mother and said, "Mother, Jillian is the only one who can help."

I felt the mother's pain as she told me Aimee was now institutionalized under close psychiatric care. She asked if I would be willing to write to her daughter. At this date, two letters have gone back and forth. I sense the beginning of healing as Aimee opens up to someone whom she feels can understand.

I must confess that I feel devastated when I hear these stories of such intense pain and anguish I've told here. And I'm sorry that these three happen to involve abuse by people who were church-related. But after all, this is where my music ministry takes place, and it's often people like these who talk to me.

It is hard to imagine such things happen in church circles.

It's like the shock I expressed to my parents when I told them during the first few weeks after adoption about being locked out in the dark by a foster father. I said to them in amazement, "And he was a policeman!" We don't expect to be betrayed by people in places of authority or power or prestige.

Fortunately, not all stories involve sexual abuse. But abuse is abuse, whatever form it takes. And not every story I hear is as intense as these I've just related. But pain from any cause is still pain and needs care and attention.

I'm not writing this book or conducting a music ministry to become famous. I'd rather be at an altar of prayer where two teenaged girls find hope and joy in Christ as they gain release from their past. But I hope my witness—sung, spoken, or written—will help bring healing wherever it's heard or read.

Social worker and psychotherapist, Linda T. Sanford, in her book *Strong at the Broken Places*, helps us understand how people who have been wounded so badly can be healed. She shares many interviews with people who were abused in childhood but grew to be emotionally healthy adults. All of these people wanted others to know that even given a rough childhood, a normal adult life is possible. Linda Sanford's message is that in the very places in our lives where we have been broken, we can mend and then have the strength to help others who are broken.

Corrie ten Boom, the Christian Dutch woman whose family hid Jews from the Nazis and who finally ended up in a death camp herself, related a similar story of strength in brokenness. She lost her family, but not her faith in God. And her testimony years later was, "There is no pit that he is not deeper still."

These women are saying that even broken, battered victims can recover and lead positive, productive adult lives. The human spirit can take a lot and still survive. And not only survive; by the grace of God, those who have suffered abuse can become strong in the broken places and in turn help others out of their pit. I, too, want people to know that if by God's grace I can make it, they can as well.

13

Pressing On in Love

"Praise the Lord, O my soul,
and forget not all his benefits—who forgives all your sins
and heals all your diseases, who redeems your life from the pit
and crowns you with love and compassion,
who satisfies your desires with good things."Psalm 103:2–5

W hy should I put you on the Diadem record-
ing label?" Vice president of the company, Larry Day, shot
the question at me as I sat with my producer, across from
him. With a sweep of his hand, he pointed to the shelves of
tapes from singers he had rejected. He was probing my confidence and feelings about myself.

Many thoughts rushed through my mind. What does he
really want to know? Should I mention the wide range of
my voice or my concerts and speaking engagements all
across the country? He should know about my TV appearances, my radio interviews, and my work with World Vision.

With a fresh sense of God's inner direction I answered his

question, also mentioning briefly my story of abandonment, abuse, and healing, as well as my search for my birth family. And I tried to show him that my goal in life now is to serve the Lord.

Larry seemed impressed, even slightly excited. But I had no demo (demonstration tape) to play for him. I didn't want to offer him my first album, because I felt I could do so much better than that early effort.

"I can't make any commitment, but I'd like to attend one of your concerts when you're near home here in Nashville," Larry finally said.

Following that concert he offered me studio time to produce a demo so that the company could make a decision. It was a positive one.

After months of searching out the best new songs and excellent backup singers, instrumentalists, engineers, and studio facilities, we did the recording, the mixing, the final polishing. It took others six more weeks to make the master disk, and then the first tapes and CDs for the market. Finally, thanks to many people and to Mark, my producer, my 1990 album *Defender*, was ready.

In my almost eighteen months in Nashville prior to the album's release, even more important things were happening. I was finding strong inner support as I met fellow believers and became established in my local church. It was a good feeling to have those I needed to be accountable to— a pastor, friends, mature counselors.

When I became ill on a previous visit to the city before I moved here, the church had provided an apartment in which to recover and compassionate persons to care for me. God's people are wonderful everywhere in the world! Now, since the release of the album and the increase in number and size of concerts, more good things are happening to me.

I'm thankful I have survived so much, especially in my adult life. God has been my preserver and provider. He has enabled me to buy and customize a new townhouse that serves as my office and a refuge after traveling. China Doll,

132   *Please, Somebody Love Me!*

my wrinkled shar-pei dog and Minx, my not-so-little bull mastiff, make excellent alarms, protectors, and friends.

My home church and pastor in Nashville cared enough about me to want the church board to interview both me and Mark and to hear our testimonies. They offered an accountability relationship for my ministry and in turn agreed to be supportive and encouraging in prayer. Then, before the entire congregation, I was given what the denomination calls a Local Minister's License, intended to verify that I am in good standing and accountable to the church. It means that others have a reference point for my spiritual life and practice.

New ways and places to tell my story began to develop. One weekend of travel included a singles' meeting, three Sunday morning concerts, and an appearance on Dr. Richard Jackson's TV program, "Coffee with the Pastor"—all at the huge North Phoenix Baptist Church. Afterward, one of the phone calls I received came from the national publication, *Christian Single.* I was happy to give them a personality profile article for the magazine.

Another time, I was in concert at Bethany Church of the Nazarene in Oklahoma City, the largest church in the denomination. Afterward, Susie Shellenberger of Focus on the Family's new *Brio* magazine called. We arranged for a later interview time for a feature cover story for the May, 1991, issue.

I am learning more and more of the value of friendships after missing out on them so much in my teens.

It was a typically windy day in Chicago, and I was at TV Channel 38 to participate in a telethon. All the guests were gathering and being made up for the camera. It was then that I met singing star Anita Bryant. When we were introduced, we both seemed to sense we would become good friends. I spent several hours shopping with Anita that weekend and met her husband, NASA test pilot Charlie Dry. Anita and I could identify with each other through many hurts, victories, and successes. I admire her for being the survivor that she is.

I was thrilled to discover we were actually neighbors in Nashville. Anita and her husband have a place in the same townhouse complex, not many doors from mine. Mark and I enjoyed a Thanksgiving dinner at their place and we have had wonderful long talks on other occasions.

That same Chicago telethon also gave me opportunity to renew a friendship I had developed with producer Shirley Dougan. She had moved from an East Coast cable network where I have performed to join the staff of Jerry Rose, president of the National Religious Broadcasters.

I am making some good friends from coast to coast. For instance, it's always a happy day for me when I am booked for concerts in the San Francisco Bay area. I like the city, but what I like best is being able to spend time with my girlfriend Vonda Haus of Channel 65, where I've appeared. Whether it's Anita, Shirley, Vonda, or others I may count as special friends—these people are God's unusually good gifts of encouragement.

One afternoon I was busy getting ready for a tour in Minnesota and Wisconsin when that ever-insistent phone rang. I was surprised but delighted to hear from my friend, David Clydesdale, who has arranged many well-known songs for Sandi Patti.

"Jillian, what are you doing next Monday?" That was the Monday before Christmas he was asking about. I told him of my planned twelve-day tour.

"Oh, what am I going to do? I had hoped to get you to cohost a special Christmas program at the Tennessee Baptist Children's Home. Amy Grant will be performing as well."

This opportunity to be with the children was one I couldn't turn down, even though it meant a special one-day flight back. My manager, John Taylor, picked me up at the airport the evening I returned so I could make a hurried change for the Christmas event at the children's home just outside Nashville. I'm sure I was as excited thinking about the event as the children were.

That night I told my story to the children and sang some

Please, Somebody Love Me!

of the songs from my album. About a hundred of the children sat on the floor around me, and another two hundred were at the banquet tables. They gave me their full attention while I told them of being a foster child, feeling like an orphan myself, moving from home to home.

I told those precious children how as a little girl at Christmastime I used to dream of a knight in shining armor riding in on his white horse to rescue me. I expected him to take me to a castle far away. "Well," I told them, "my knight finally came. But he didn't arrive on a beautiful horse; he came as a baby in a manger to grow up and be the Savior for all who accept him. He died on the cross and rose from the grave and said he would provide a home for us. Tonight we all have a forever home prepared for us."

At the end of the evening I leaned over to John Taylor and said, "Wouldn't it be wonderful if I could take a little boy or girl home, like David Clydesdale and his wife do each Christmas?"

When the director of the nine Baptist homes in Tennessee thanked me for appearing, I asked him if I could take one of the children home. He said that such arrangements usually involve a lot of red tape, but he'd see what he could do.

While I was back on my Minnesota tour, I received a call confirming that I could take a twelve-year-old girl named Susie to my home for a few days between Christmas and New Year's Day. Susie had been abandoned by her parents after suffering abuse by her father and brothers as well as beatings by her mother.

We had three exciting days together as Mark helped me take her to a movie, to different eating places, and to the eighth floor of the United Artists building for a view of the city. There she also saw a record being produced and met the staff at Diadem where I record.

Susie was almost too polite, unable to express what she wanted to eat or do. But gradually she opened up a little about her past abuse. She said she hoped to be adopted some day and have her "forever home" too.

Concerts in Dallas were ahead on the weekend, so Mark

and I took Susie to the children's home before my afternoon flight. Silence hovered over us on the drive there. We were teary-eyed as we drove up to the cottage where Susie lived with fourteen girls and boys and her house parents. I walked her inside; we said our good-byes, and I gave her a big hug. I told her we hoped to see her again and returned to the car.

As I was getting into the car I heard her cottage door open. Susie ran into my arms, sobbing, and held on around my neck. When I looked up and saw tears in Mark's eyes, too, I found it hard to keep from breaking down completely. When I got back from Dallas there was a message on my answering machine from Susie saying, "Jillian, I love you and miss you." I hope we can get together again soon.

Over the past few years, I have visited with scores of pastors and listened to hundreds of people share their personal pain. As a result, I understand much better what happened to me as a child. I also have some ideas for how churches can respond compassionately to the variety of hurts people experience. I'd like to see churches and their leadership take at least six steps:

1. *Do more to prepare couples for marriage and to provide solutions for conflict where divorce threatens.* The breakup of my birth parents' marriage was the first in the series of events that nearly destroyed my life. And I have learned that the breakup of the original family unit always damages children to a lesser or greater degree—whether they end up in foster care, as I did, in a single-parent home, or in a "blended" family. For this reason alone, I believe churches can never work too hard to stress the importance of marriage and to help families stay together.

2. *Help more Christian families prepare to receive foster children.* Rather than cursing the darkness of some foster care, I believe Christians should light a candle of love by opening their homes to children in need of foster care. By providing a frightened, lonely child with a refuge of peace and stability, a place where moral and physical safety are certain, Chris-

　　　　　　　　　　Please, Somebody Love Me!

tians have the opportunity to prevent the kind of suffering I went through as a young child.

3. *Educate church members to recognize the symptoms of abuse and help children recover.* In part, this means resisting the "it's not my business" impulse. People also need to understand the results of abuse. Self-hate, the inability to accept love, an attitude of distrust, manipulative behavior, or even violent outbursts can reflect a background of childhood abuse. As my adoptive parents learned, helping a child handle this legacy of pain takes deep caring and patient involvement.

4. *Prepare the church family to understand and work with adults who are living out the results of their early abuse.* For example a woman who was abused as a child will often grow up believing that abuse is what she deserves—or that it is the only form of attention she can get. She may even confuse abuse with love. As a result, unless she receives help, she is likely to find herself in one abusive situation after another.

Most Christians could benefit from familiarity with recent writings on the subject of codependency that show how the abused often become "enablers" for abusers. Christians also need to understand that abuse comes in many forms—verbal, emotional, or physical—and can be directed toward the elderly as well as toward children, spouses, and dates.

In most churches, child abuse and date or spouse battering have been discussed only informally and spasmodically. As a result, church members tend to be just as ignorant about these forms of abuse as the general population. For instance, many church people find it difficult to believe a woman who says she is being abused. They think she is just angry at her husband or has done something wrong herself. And Christians persist in thinking, "It couldn't happen in *our* church."

5. *Help pastors become more aware of abuse and how to deal with it.* Before church members will be able to help abused children or adults, I believe pastors will have to lead the way. Pastors must come to terms with the fact that abuse does happen—even among Christians—and understand its effects.

In the case of one couple I know well, the husband was

emotionally hurtful and making physically/sexually abusive demands on his wife. When she sought help from the pastor who had married them, he said the husband was just being lustful toward his wife and implied that what he was doing was appropriate behavior in marriage. When the husband refused to join his wife for professional counseling, the marriage dissolved.

In particular, then, pastors must be alert to the possibility of abuse in Christian homes. James and Phyllis Alsdurf in their book, *Battered into Submission,* say that while Christian marriages have a lower incidence of abuse, it does occur among Christians. They estimate that ten out of sixty married women in a church suffer verbal and emotional abuse and that two or three will be physically abused.

They also suggest that pastors can include in public prayer the subject of violence in the home where women and boys and girls may be suffering from it. Such leadership can lift the awareness of the congregation and help victims believe a pastor does care and might listen if they approached him or her.

Pastors need to be aware of date battering, in addition to other forms of abuse. In a study done at Oregon State University a few years ago, nearly one-fourth of the students questioned said they experienced kicking, biting, shoving or slapping during courtship and live-in relationships. In a Minnesota study, 21 percent of the students questioned experienced violence within their relationships, and in Arizona, 60 percent said it was part of their dating life.

And please don't think date battering won't happen to youth in your church. It happened to me. My youth intern pastor at the time didn't understand. He tried to bridge what he thought was a communication gap between my batterer, Chris, and me. In addition to providing the more complete training most pastoral staff members need in this field, why can't churches develop youth classes for teaching more about the dynamics of male-female relationships? It is during the dating period that patterns for marital abuse are set.

6. *Finally, I'd like to say to pastors and the entire church family*

regarding the abused: Believe them when they come to you! Pray with them. Offer them choices, and encourage them to take action. Help them find supporting, caring friends and professional counseling. Remind them that God loves them and does not want them to suffer abuse.

I have so much respect for my pastor, Millard Reed, who provides such fine support in this area. How grateful I am for a home base where the staff is willing to work through the issues of abuse and victimization. Such help can make all the difference in the lives of teens and adults hidden in our churches who are suffering and need help.

I remember Janine, who came up to me after a service in a large southern city. She and her husband were sponsors of the high-school group.

"Jillian, I want you to know what happened in my life as a result of your concert here three months ago. My father was an alcoholic, and my mother put up with it. Aside from the physical abuse we received when Dad was drunk, we lost out on most of the common things other families enjoy —like eating meals together or going on family outings. He died when he was in his forties, and my mother died a short time later.

"For a long time I was unaware of the anger that ate at me inside. I compensated for the lack of love in my childhood by trying to gain approval every way I could as an adult. Even lately, if there were to be refreshments for the youth (or any group at church) and I was asked to pick them up, I would not let anyone repay me for them. I wanted to be the 'good' person, loved and liked. But deep inside I was sure no one could ever like me.

"But Jillian, when you were here last time, I turned all my past and my unhealthy adult responses over to the Lord. I forgave those in my past—even though some are dead. And I've learned to be transparent about myself and the things that have happened to me. Best of all, because I am open with the high schoolers, they are now able to open up to me about their hurts. And we've had some great steps of faith and decisions among them in the last few weeks!"

What a lesson on what transparency will do for our lives

and in our relationships with each other—if we can only learn to stop seeking each other's approval so much and just be who we are in Christ!

Victims of date and spouse abuse need teaching on love and forgiveness. How desperately they need to hear of the infinite worth of a human being—made so beautifully clear in Jesus' death on the cross for every person. For the abused person, knowing "I am supremely valued" by the One whose love never changes can only bring hope, stability, and confidence.

Unconditional love and acceptance needs to be genuinely present in a church so the abused can readily sense it. Professional counselors are needed on staff in larger churches; smaller churches can use a referral system. Also well-trained lay counselors and support groups composed of other abused persons can be useful to many who are in pain.

As I have been given the privilege, through my concerts and in my personal life, to minister to people in pain, I have come to appreciate anew the people who have helped me through my own pain. In particular, I have developed a new appreciation for my adoptive family. They provided me with the things that really matter in life—not just a home, food, clothing, and shelter, but also stable, steady, patient care with love. And by introducing me to Jesus Christ, they brought me into the greatest family of all, the family of God. His people are everywhere. Long after my parents are gone, I will still be a member of the family of faith.

Could I have missed all this? Who knows what might have been—if my birth family had not split up . . . if I had not been placed in foster homes . . . if Mom and Dad had not adopted me. I do know that God loved me from the beginning and has brought me, step by step, to where I am today. Because of what he has already done in my life, I can trust him for my future.

needed such a person. When there was nothing cohesive or constant, she had held my life together.

Two thousand miles separated us, but by phone I was able to reach out and touch her again. Our excitement was mutual. I told her how much she had meant to me and then related something of my present life. She exclaimed, "Jillian, you're a star. I always knew you had it in you!"

That first phone call didn't satisfy my longing to assure myself I had really found Mrs. Schlesinger. Hearing her voice, plus finding a children's book she had signed and given me when I was a little girl, started bringing my memories of her into focus. It had always seemed so much safer to keep those memories of her and my early childhood in the guarded places of my mind. But now they were dancing all around me, and I felt good about them.

I found myself looking for any excuse to go back to Los Angeles. And three different times I flew there with arrangements all made to see her. But each time I became ill. Twice, I developed high fevers that forced me to return home immediately. A third time I became violently sick to my stomach.

Why did I get so sick each time? Was it because Mrs. Schlesinger had been so important to me in those early years? She certainly was the only stable, caring person in my life when there was no one else I could trust or count on. Or was my planned meeting with her a reminder of others who had failed me? Subconsciously, I must have felt that I was going back in time, experiencing again those early emotional stresses. In the face of such emotional upheaval, my body must have naturally rebelled.

Now once more, realizing that this book was almost finalized and the publishing contract signed, I knew it was my last chance to see her before its release.

Fortunately, on this trip to Los Angeles I had made arrangements to stay with some friends. They understood my feelings and encouraged me to fulfill my dream. On my arrival I called Mrs. Schlesinger and set up our meeting for the last day before my departure home.

Finally, with great expectation on my part, the day came. It was warm and sunny as my friends drove me to Mrs. Schlesinger's neighborhood. As we arrived in front of her house, I took a long, deep breath. Though anxiety about this meeting closed my eyes to some things around me, I couldn't miss her yard, which was full of tropical flowers and trees.

My friends escorted me to the door with cameras ready so I'd have pictures to remind me of this special moment. But it was not an easy walk to take. I remembered going up too many walkways—to foster homes and "forever" homes.

The doorbell responded to my hesitant touch. I felt like a little girl. I had stepped back in time. But Mrs. Schlesinger didn't know me at first. Her first words when she opened the door were, "Which one is Jillian?"

I stepped forward. "Oh, my word," she said, "you are so big and beautiful." We clinched in a big hug.

Her observation was the reverse of mine. I remembered her as being such a tall lady. Now, with the heels I wore, I stood four or five inches taller than she. Her nicely styled gray hair, the beautiful necklace she wore, and her paisley print outfit presented her as an attractive person. Her low-pitched voice and precise manner of speaking revealed her to be an educated, cultured lady.

My friends stayed only a few moments before politely taking their leave so we could be alone.

When they were gone, Mrs. Schlesinger walked me into the dining room where she had prepared a lovely table of fresh fruit and salad. As she and I sat across from each other and began to talk, I assured her of my fond memories and was able to express my deep feelings for her.

She asked about things I might have remembered. When I described my memories, she confirmed many of the foster homes and family names as well as places we went together and schools I attended. We laughed together remembering the old red station wagon in which she took me to the park. The back of that car was always filled with toys.

Then she asked me if I remembered any abuse. "Yes," I said, but I wanted to say, "How could I forget?"

She asked several other questions, her blue eyes fixed on

my face. The one I remember most was, "Did you feel you had it rough?"

I answered, "yes," not really knowing how to answer, but feeling all the justification in the world for that one word.

"Well, you didn't," she fired back. "You really had it quite good. Many, many children have suffered more in our system. We had no way of knowing what you children were really going through. Each foster family was interviewed and carefully selected. I'm very sorry we couldn't have had more control. In many cases we didn't know the details of what happened until years later."

At first her words confused and angered me. Then I realized she was trying to tell me there were many situations from which the children never did recover. It seemed that my presence actually shocked her, so great was the contrast from what she knew had happened to many abandoned children.

Then on a more tender, personal note she added, "You were a darling little girl. Everyone at the agency loved you. You were so charming, and you loved to entertain us."

When she understood some of the things that had happened to me in my foster homes and in later years and yet saw that I had made it, she asked, "How did you survive so well? So many don't come through it."

She became very quiet when I began to tell her about my emotional healing and all that Jesus Christ had done in my life. It was my opportunity to answer her question in the only way I could do it justice—an open witnessing to what God can do in a life.

We had so little time before my friends arrived to take me to the airport. But this reunion after twenty-two years helped me tie off some more loose threads in the fabric of my life. I held my head high and controlled the tears that so badly wanted to gush out. I hugged her good-bye and invited her to my next concert in Los Angeles. With an air of excitement she accepted my invitation.

As I stepped away from the house I found it harder and harder to control all the emotions swirling inside me. Once inside the car, I exploded with uncontrollable tears—my

Please, Somebody Love Me!

whole body convulsed with inner wrenchings—while my mind tried hard to sort out all I was feeling.

How could I pretend this meeting was as special for Mrs. Schlesinger as it was for me? To me, that woman had been everything—my whole world, my safe place, my friend. But I had only been one of many who ran down the hallway, excited to meet her outstretched arms. Still, she had seemed so happy to see me. . . .

This could not be good-bye. It was a start. A new beginning. The reopening of lost pages in the story of my life. Mrs. Schlesinger had been to me the memory of a mother, the mother I never had until my adoption. Now she was a real person in my life. I know I'll see her again.

A Final Note

It has been terribly painful for me to give you these pages of my life . . . to remember . . . relive what I've left behind.

But oh, the happy rewards that will be mine as you, my reader and newfound friend, find fresh hope and new strength and perhaps another new friend—my friend, Jesus. He can bring healing to your life as he has to mine. He can put back together what was broken. He can restore what was lost.

This life is but a passing moment. Tomorrow you will awake and wonder where time went. So don't wait. Begin working to accomplish your dream. Reach for the stars. Let go of your pain and let love consume your soul. Don't look back!

As you run your race, I know that my father in heaven will supply *all* your need. Press on toward the mark—full speed ahead—and allow life to reward you abundantly.

For I know so well that there *is* joy, sweet joy in the morning, as we press on together in his love.

The Plan
(written on Thanksgiving Day at age eighteen)

Far away, long ago, a child was born.
But did she know what was ahead or what was planned?
She was too young to believe
That her life was all in God's hand.

She started out not having a home,
Nothing of which she could call her own.
Families of strangers, one after another—
Who would she next call father and mother?

Along with her search was need of an identity—
Who could she trust, who could she believe?
Love never came easy, bitterness filled her heart;
She grew up not knowing how to tell them apart.

I know you still say this is all part of a plan.
Why couldn't she believe her life was all in God's hands?
It was in her eighth year she was finally accepted,
Adoption gave the meaning, she was no longer rejected.
But what about her past—it wasn't easy to forget.
If this was a plan, why did she have to pay such a debt?

She grew older; time just rolled on.
Things that were important to her were things that
    were wrong.
She wanted to win and at everything be best.
People who wanted to love her she put to the test.

Material things possessed her,
She portrayed pictures in magazines—
Outwardly beautiful, but inside you could never see.
Why such an appearance and why still hide from her past?
Inside full of painful memories; inside she couldn't last.

Jesus came to earth born of Virgin Mary,
Through life the clothes on his back
Were all that he carried.
He had no home to stay in, but traveled from city to city
Telling people about his Father,
How his love could set them free.
Jesus looked to no other images, none from magazines.
He needed nothing of material wealth,
Only his father for him to see.

Please, Somebody Love Me!

Jesus grew older; time just rolled on.
They nailed him to a cross; man did what was wrong.
But Jesus died to save us. He took all our blame.
He died for that little child's hurt,
And he died for you just the same.

I know this is a story; it may be hard to believe.
But this isn't just a story because that little girl was me.
So don't worry about what's ahead,
Don't worry about what has been planned.
Just look to God and believe
Your life is all in his hand.

Resource List

Some Books that Helped Me in My Struggle

1. Buehler, Richard. *Pain and Pretending*. Nashville: Thomas Nelson, 1988 (rev. 1990). This book is designed to help a victim learn how to lead a normal life.
2. Hemfelt, Robert, Frank Minirth, and Paul Meier. *Love Is a Choice: Recovery for Codependents*. Nashville: Thomas Nelson, 1989. This helpful, biblically sound guide on codependency and recovery makes good reading for any adult.
3. Littauer, Florence. *Help For Hurting Women*. (earlier title: *Lives on the Mend*). Dallas: Word, 1985. This is the book that initially put me on the road to emotional healing. It presents the stories of a number of women who were victims of some of life's most painful circumstances and tells how they found recovery.
4. Swindoll, Charles. *Living above the Level of Mediocrity*. Dallas: Word, 1985. This captivating book shows how to live without compromising one's values. It will challenge you to be all you can be.

Other Resources for Information and Help —Child Abuse—

1. American Medical Association and the National Association of State Boards of Education. *Code Blue: American Medical Association (AMA) Commission Report on Child Abuse*. Alexandria, VA: NASBE, 1990. Order from the NASBE at 1012 Cameron St., Alexandria, VA, 22314. 703-684-4000. Cost is $12.50.

2. Hawkins, Paula. *Children at Risk: My Fight against Child Abuse—A Personal Story and a Public Plea.* Bethesda, MD: Adler and Adler, 1986. The Senator from Florida tells of being sexually molested as a five-year-old and of her fight as an adult in public service to combat child abuse. This publication contains an extensive listing of helping agencies in all states.

3. National Center on Child Abuse and Neglect. *Catalog of Child Abuse and Neglect Publications.* Washington, D.C.: Department of Health and Human Services. The materials from the government listed in this catalog are useful to those fighting the problem, not to a victim in crisis. Some items are free; others range from one dollar up. Catalog is available at no charge from the National Center on Child Abuse and Neglect, P.O. Box 1182, Washington, D.C. 20013.

4. National Center on Child Abuse and Neglect. *Child Abuse and Neglect: A Shared Community Concern.* Washington, D.C.: U.S. Department of Health and Human Services, 1989. This thirty-one page document on defining, recognizing, preventing, and helping victims of child abuse also lists National Child Welfare Resource Centers and other state agencies and national organizations concerned with child maltreatment. It can be ordered at no charge from the above address.

5. National Center on Child Abuse and Neglect. *Executive Summary: Study of National Incidence and Prevalence of Child Abuse and Neglect.* Washington, D.C.: U.S. Department of Health and Human Services, 1988. This booklet, which includes statistical data, can be ordered from the above address.

6. Sanford, Linda. *Strong at the Broken Places: Overcoming the Trauma of Childhood Abuse.* New York: Random House, 1990. This is an especially encouraging book for the victim.

7. The C. Henry Kempe National Center for the Prevention and Treatment of Child Abuse and Neglect, 1205 Oneida St., Denver, CO 80220, 303-321-3963. They provide printed resources and help in finding support groups.

Child Abuse Hotlines

1. CHILDHELP USA, 1-800-4-A-CHILD (1-800-412-4453). National headquarters: 6463 Independence Ave., Woodland Hills, CA 91367, 818-347-7280. (This last number for informa-

tion only.) This organization provides crisis counseling for the victim. CHILDHELP's function, after the crisis of the moment, is to put the victim in touch with resources in his or her own community.

2. Clearinghouse on Child Abuse and Neglect, 703-821-2086. This is an information center.

3. National Center on Child Abuse and Neglect, 303-321-3963. This organization provides help for those fighting child abuse in society.

Spouse Abuse

1. Alsdurf, James W. and Phyllis Alsdurf. *Battered into Submission*. Downers Grove, IL: InterVarsity Press, 1984. James Alsdurf, a forensic psychologist with the Hennepin County Court Services in Minneapolis, teams with Phyllis Alsdurf, a freelance writer and former editor, to carefully survey from a Scriptural perspective the problem of the battered woman. Included is a chapter on the propriety of divorce when violence is present—a significant concern of conscience to Christians caught in the abuse cycle.

2. Martin, Grant L. *Please Don't Hurt Me: A Sensitive Look at the Growing Problem of Abuse in Christian Homes*. Wheaton, IL: Victor Books (SP Publications), 1987.

3. Fortune, Marie M. *Sexual Violence: The Unmentionable Sin— An Ethical and Pastoral Perspective*. New York: Pilgrim Press, 1983. This book is an excellent pastoral resource.

4. Fortune, Marie M. *Keeping the Faith: Questions and Answers for Abused Women*. New York: Pilgrim Press, 1987. This book, which deals with questions that plague the abused woman, contains an excellent section of suggestions for pastors and lay persons.

5. Horton, Anne L. and Judith A. Williamson. *Abuse and Religion: When Praying Isn't Enough*. Lexington, MA: Lexington Books, 1988. Chapters are written by a variety of authors from differing backgrounds. This study book for clergy and other helping professionals covers abuse of all kinds.

6. Pellauer, Mary D., Barbara Chester and Jane Boya. *Sexual Assault and Abuse: A Handbook for Clergy and Religious Professionals*. New York: Harper and Row, 1987. This handbook

provides help for recognizing the patterns, understanding the issues, and responding with compassion.

Spouse Abuse Hotlines

1. Domestic Violence Hotline, 1-800-333-SAFE(7233). This organization provides crisis counseling and referrals to shelters, counseling, legal help, and support groups. (Date abuse is considered a form of domestic violence.)

For Adoptees

Many parents—both adoptive and birth parents, prefer that there be no contact between adopted children and the birth family. And many adoptees have no desire to search for their roots. But for those who do, for medical reasons or other, the following information is provided:

1. ALMA (Adoptees Liberty Movement Association), P.O. Box 154, Washington Bridge Station, New York, NY 10033. 212-581-1568. This organization provides adoptees with help in searching for their birth families.
2. Soundex Reunion Registry, P.O. Box 2312, Carson City, NV 89702. 702-882-7755. This is not a search-help agency, but an informational registry to help family members (not just adopted ones) find each other. It is open from 9:00 A.M. to 5:00 P.M. PST.
3. Salvation Army. Although the Salvation Army as a whole is no longer active in adoption searches, some local Army units have personnel who can suggest procedures to aid in search.

Some Key Statistics on Abuse*

1. Every year, more than two million children and adolescents are reported abused or neglected.
2. Five hundred thousand children and adolescents are placed in foster homes or institutions each year.
3. One in four girls and one in eight boys will be abused in some way by the time they are eighteen.
4. The average age of a victim of child abuse is seven.
5. In the U.S., a woman is battered by her partner every fifteen seconds.

6. Battering accounts for 20 percent of emergency room visits and 25 percent of suicide attempts by women.
7. It is estimated that between 20 percent and 52 percent of high-school and college-age dating couples have engaged in physical abuse.

*The source for items 1 and 2 is the AMA's *Code Blue*, listed early. The source for item 3 is clinical psychologist Cynthia Stout. The source for item 4 is *Combatting Child Abuse Across America* (Childhelp USA). The source for items 5 through 7 is the Portland (Oregon) Women's Crisis Line.

Jillian Ryan is a Christian recording artist who resides in Phoenix, Arizona, with her husband, Ron Whitaker.

Joseph A. Ryan is Jillian's adoptive father, a freelance writer, and the author of *The Remarriage Handbook for the Widowed*.

Inquiries regarding concerts and speaking availability may be made by contacting:

Jillian Ministries
8711 East Pinnacle Pk. Rd. #182
Scottsdale, AZ 85255
(602) 502-5357